AMERICA'S BOUNTY

*Down-To-Earth Foods
From the Garden, Orchard,
Field, River and Ocean*

KATHY BLAKE

SMITHMARK

This edition published by SMITHMARK Publishers Inc., 16 East 32nd Street, New York, NY 10016

SMITHMARK books are available for bulk purchase for sales promotion and premium use. For details write or call the manager of special sales, SMITHMARK Publishers Inc., 16 East 32nd Street, New York, NY 10016; (212) 532-6600

This book was designed and produced by Todtri Productions Limited P.O. Box 20058 New York, NY 10023-1482

Printed and bound in Singapore

Library of Congress Catalog Card Number 95-067560

ISBN 0-8317-8173-4

Author: Kathy Blake

Producer: Robert M. Tod
Book Designer: Mark Weinberg
Production Coordinator: Heather Weigel
Photo Editors: Edward Douglas, Ede Rothaus
Editors: Don Kennison, Shawna Kimber, Linda Greer
Typesetting: Command-O, NYC

PHOTO CREDITS

Photographic Source/Page Number

Charles Braswell Jr. 7, 13, 22-23, 100-101, 107, 118

Bullaty Lomeo 19

Dembinsky Photo Associates
Willard Clay 26-27, 84-85
Sharon Cummings 72-73
Darrell Gulin 8-9
Doug Locke 4-5
Gary Meszaros 104-105
G. Alan Nelson 83

Envision
Priscilla Connell 36-37
Dennis Galante 42-43, 74-75, 90-91, 96-97, 102-103
Wolfgang Hoffmann 21
Peter Johansky 66
Ted Morrison 52
Steven Mark Needham 12, 32, 39, 46, 48, 54, 58-59, 60, 63, 70, 76-77, 80-81, 86, 111, 112, 119
Rick Osentoski 18, 49, 94
Overseas 30, 34-35, 93
Amy Reichman 122

Lois Ellen Frank 69, 98, 114-115

Adam Jones 24-25, 106, 123, 127

New England Stock Photo
Roger Bickel 88-89
Carol Christensen 79
Robert Deschene 44
Fred M. Dole 38
John D. Harper 29
Margot Taussig Pinkerton 62
Dave Rusk 126
Kevin Shields 64-65, 68
W.J. Talarowski 40-41

Zeva Oelbaum 6, 117, 124-125

Nancy Palubniak 16-17, 71, 113, 116

Photo/Nats Jennifer Graylock 50-51

Picture Perfect USA
William D. Adams 15
Steve Bentsen 99
Jaimie Blandford 78
Linda Burgess 120-121
Robert Dawson 82
John Farnham 10
John Glover 108
Alan K. Mallams 53
Joe McDonald 14
Robert Pollock 92
Wayne Shields 56-57
Ron Spomer 45

CONTENTS

INTRODUCTION

From mountains and plains, lakes and seas; from tiny gardens and massive ranches, America's bounteous harvest provides a year-round abundance. The recipes and photographs in this book invoke America's bounty and offer some familiar and some innovative ways to incorporate fresh ingredients into meals for your family and friends.

Favorite dishes are included here from various regions of the country—dishes that were based on traditional preparations from immigrants' homelands in Europe, Britain, Africa, Asia, and beyond and have evolved through decades and even centuries, and still remain mainstays of daily and celebratory menus.

You're sure to discover recipes in this book that will soon become favorites in your home. From the deep South come Okra-Tomato Stew and Shrimp Creole; traditional Maryland Crabcakes and Chicken Pot Pies hale from the North; the plains and dairy farms of the great Midwest offer Wisconsin Cheese Fondue and Minnesota Wild Rice Soup, while the multicultural West gives us Chicken Chorizo, Texas-Style Ribs, and San Francisco Tuna Steaks.

As you browse through the recipes and admire the photographs offered here, you will experience a renewed appreciation for America's Bounty.

FROM THE GARDEN

*T*illing, planting, tending and harvesting are activities that people have enjoyed and have had a need to do, whether for sustenance or psychic satisfaction, since prehistoric times. Seeing tender plants emerge from black earth and grow to fruition, then taking the vegetables to the table or preparing them for canning are rewarding on many levels.

Today, America is checkered with backyard gardens where fresh lettuces, herbs, tomatoes, cucumbers, squashes and other spring, summer and autumn favorites grow in profusion. Meanwhile, farmers cultivate vast areas in all regions of America, providing food for the world. America's bounty includes a wealth of beautiful shapes and a rainbow of colors in the forms of vegetables. During any season of the year, we can fill cornucopias with an astonishing array of American-grown produce.

Whether harvested from a home garden, purchased directly from farmers or from supermarkets, fresh and preserved vegetables add color, flavor and nutrition to our menus. This chapter will introduce new ways to prepare old favorites and perhaps inspire you with ways to present exotic new salads and vegetable dishes to your family.

DILLED CUCUMBERS

1 cup water
1/4 cup white vinegar
2 tablespoons sugar
1 tablespoon fresh dill, chopped
2 cucumbers, peeled and thinly sliced
1 slice onion, about 1/4-inch thick

In a glass or ceramic bowl, stir together the water, vinegar, sugar, and dill. Add the cucumbers and onion; stir; refrigerate for one hour. Remove the onion; serve.

Makes 4 servings

SHREDDED CUCUMBER SALAD WITH CHIVE VINAIGRETTE

VINAIGRETTE:
2 tablespoons white wine vinegar
2 tablespoons olive oil
1 tablespoon Dijon mustard
1 tablespoon minced chives
2 teaspoons sugar
1/4 teaspoon salt

SALAD:
4 cucumbers, peeled and seeded
1 carrot
1/2 green pepper

Prepare the vinaigrette: Place all ingredients in a jar, cover and shake vigorously; set aside.

Prepare the salad: With a food processor or a large grater, shred the cucumbers and carrot into a large bowl. Cut or shred green pepper into fine slivers and add to bowl. Toss the vinaigrette and salad together just before serving.

Makes 4 to 6 servings

What is paradise? but a garden, an orchard of trees and herbs full of pleasure and nothing there but delights.

WILLIAM LAWSON

RED PEPPER-
BROCCOLI SALAD

DRESSING:
2 tablespoons vegetable or olive oil
2 tablespoons lemon juice
1/4 teaspoon salt

SALAD:
1 red bell pepper
1 head broccoli
1/4 cup chopped red onion

Prepare the dressing: Pour all ingredients into a jar, cover and shake well; set aside.

Prepare the salad: Roast the red pepper by hold-ing it with tongs over a flame, turning until the entire surface is blackened and blistered. Place the pepper in a paper bag to cool, then rub the skin off. Cut the pepper open, remove the seeds and cut it into thin slices.

Peel the hard skin off the stem of the broccoli, then cut the stem crosswise into rounds and cut the head into florets. Blanch the broccoli in boil-ing water for a few seconds, or until it turns bright green. Pour it into a colander to drain, then immerse in cold water; drain well.

Put the broccoli in a salad bowl, sprinkle with onion, then top with red pepper slices. Pour the reserved dressing over the salad; toss; refrigerate for no longer than one hour. Toss again just before serving.

Makes 4 to 6 servings

★ ★

ROASTED VEGETABLE-PASTA SALAD

1 small eggplant
2 zucchini
1 red pepper, seeded
1 green pepper, seeded
1 medium yellow onion
1/4 cup olive oil
2 tablespoons balsamic vinegar
1/2 teaspoon salt
1/4 teaspoon pepper
12 ounces pasta, such as rotelle, radiatore, or medium shells
2 tomatoes, chopped
1 tablespoon chopped fresh basil
(or 1 teaspoon dried basil)

Peel the eggplant and cut into strips about 2 inches long and 1/2-inch wide; place in a colander and sprinkle with salt; allow to drain 30 minutes. Heat the oven to 400° F. Meanwhile, cut the zucchini, red pepper, green pepper, and onion into matchstick-size pieces. Rinse the eggplant and drain well. Spread all the vegetables, except the tomato, on a large baking sheet with a rim. Sprinkle the vegetables with oil, vinegar, salt, and pepper; bake 20 minutes, stirring twice, or until all the vegetables are tender and beginning to brown. Set aside to cool.

Prepare pasta according to package directions; drain and pour into salad bowl. Toss the warm pasta with vegetables, tomatoes, and basil. Serve warm or at room temperature.

Makes 8 servings

STAR-SPANGLED SPINACH SALAD

DRESSING:
1/2 cup orange juice
1/4 cup vegetable or olive oil

1/4 cup honey
2 tablespoons mustard
2 tablespoons grated onion
1/4 teaspoon salt
1/4 teaspoon pepper

SALAD:
4 cups young spinach leaves, stems removed and washed well
2 star fruit, cut crosswise into 1/4-inch slices

Prepare the dressing: Place all dressing ingredients in a jar, cover and shake vigorously; set aside.

Prepare the salad: Toss spinach and star fruit together in a salad bowl. Just before serving, pour about a third of the dressing over the salad and toss again. Serve immediately and pass the remaining dressing.

Makes 4 servings

CHEESY MASHED POTATO TART

2 1/2 pounds russet potatoes
1/2 cup milk or buttermilk
2 tablespoons flour
2 tablespoons butter or margarine
1/2 cup chopped onion
4 slices bacon, cooked and crumbled
1 cup (about 4 ounces) shredded cheese, such as Cheddar, Swiss, or Muenster

Boil the potatoes until tender, about 30 minutes; peel and mash, gradually adding milk and flour until thoroughly mashed. Heat oven to 400° F. Place butter or margarine in a 10-inch cast iron skillet or glass pie pan, then place in oven until butter is bubbling and beginning to brown. While the butter is very hot, spread the mashed potatoes in the skillet. Sprinkle with onion, bacon and cheese. Return skillet to oven and bake 30 minutes, or until the cheese is bubbly and a brown crust appears around the potatoes. Serve hot, cut into wedges.

Makes 6 servings

At midmorning, just as the sun has dried the dew from the herbs, harvest lemon verbena, cinnamon basil, peppermint or spearmint. Place the herb of your choice in a glass quart jar, then fill the jar with white sugar and cover tightly. Leave in a cool, dark place for at least a week and up to three weeks, then remove the herb from the sugar, which will be deliciously scented and ready to use in sugar cookies, iced tea, or to top oatmeal.

FRESH SALSA

1 tomato, chopped

1/2 cup chopped tomatillos

1/2 cup chopped red onion

1 clove garlic, chopped fine

2 tablespoons chopped cilantro or flat leaf parsley

1 jalapeño pepper, seeded and chopped fine

1/2 teaspoon salt

Stir all ingredients together in a bowl. Cover and refrigerate for at least one hour and up to one week. Serve with scrambled eggs, tacos, hot dogs, grilled meats, or macaroni and cheese.

Makes 2 cups

VERY SWEET POTATO PUDDING

5 medium sweet potatoes

1 cup sugar

1 cup milk

1/2 cup butter or margarine

4 eggs, lightly beaten

1 small can crushed pineapple (do not drain)

1/2 cup grated sweetened coconut (optional)

1/2 cup chopped pecans or walnuts

Heat oven to 350° F. Boil the potatoes until soft, about 30 minutes; peel and mash. Stir in sugar, milk, butter or margarine, eggs, pineapple, and coconut, if using. Grease a 2-quart casserole and pour potato mixture into it. Sprinkle with nuts. Bake 30 minutes, or until set.

Makes 6 servings

LEFT: The dressings for Spring Green Beans and New Potatoes (page 16) and Star-Spangled Spinach Salad (page 11) are joined by Fresh Salsa (above).

OKRA-TOMATO CREOLE

1 (14-ounce) can chopped tomatoes (do not drain)

1 pound fresh okra, cut into rounds

3 stalks celery, chopped

1 medium onion, chopped

1 green pepper, seeded and chopped

3 tablespoons Worcestershire sauce

1 bay leaf

1/2 teaspoon dried oregano

4 strips bacon, cooked and crumbled

Mix all ingredients in a 2-quart saucepan. Bring to a boil, reduce heat, and simmer, uncovered, for one hour. Serve with ham or fried chicken.

Makes 6 servings

Braid lengths of rough jute rope, then entwine fragrant green- and gray-leafed herbs and colorful flowers from your garden in the braid to hang and scent any room of your home.

FRIED GREEN TOMATOES

3 large green tomatoes
1/2 cup yellow cornmeal
1/4 teaspoon salt
dash pepper
vegetable oil or bacon fat for shallow frying

Slice tomatoes 1/2-inch thick. In a shallow bowl, stir together cornmeal, salt, and pepper. Heat about 1/2-inch oil or fat in a large, heavy skillet over medium heat. Dip each tomato slice in cornmeal then into hot oil and fry until brown on both sides, turning once.

Makes 6 servings

BLACK-EYED PEA SOUP

1 cup uncooked rice
1 cup water
2 cups tomato juice
1 medium onion, chopped
1 tablespoon Worcestershire sauce
1/4 teaspoon red pepper sauce
4 slices bacon, cooked and crumbled, or
1/2 cup chopped ham
1 (15-ounce) can black-eyed peas, drained and rinsed
1 cup (about 4 ounces) shredded Monterey Jack cheese
with hot chilies

In a large saucepan, stir together rice, water, tomato juice, onion, Worcestershire sauce, and red pepper sauce. Bring to a boil; reduce heat, cover and simmer on lowest heat 20 minutes. Add bacon, peas and cheese; stir well and heat thoroughly before serving. (If the soup is too thick, add more water or tomato juice.)

Makes 6 servings

SPRING
GREEN BEANS
AND
NEW POTATOES

DRESSING:
1 cup plain yogurt
1 tablespoon olive oil
1/2 teaspoon salt
1/2 teaspoon ground cumin
dash black pepper, or more to taste

VEGETABLES:
2 pounds small red potatoes
1 pound fresh green beans, cut into
1-inch lengths
10 green onions, cut into 1-inch lengths,
including some green

Prepare the dressing: In a small bowl, stir together all ingredients; set aside.

Prepare the vegetables: Bring a large pan of water to a full boil and add potatoes and green beans; simmer until tender, about 20 minutes. Drain and pour into a large bowl. Add green onions and pour dressing over all. Toss gently to coat vegetables, and serve warm.

Makes 6 servings

YANKEE CORN CHOWDER

2 cups water

1/2 cup chopped onion

1/2 cup russet potato, peeled and diced

1/2 cup chopped celery with some leaves

1/4 cup chopped parsley

2 cups milk

1 teaspoon salt

1 can (15 ounces) niblet corn, drained

In a medium saucepan, bring water to a boil and cook onion, potato, celery, and parsley for 15 minutes or until tender. Add milk and salt and heat just to boiling; stir in corn and heat again, stirring. Sprinkle each serving with additional parsley, if desired.

Makes 6 servings

LEFT: Yankee Corn Chowder

THREE GREENS SOUP

3 tablespoons butter or margarine

3 tablespoons flour

1 teaspoon salt

1 teaspoon turmeric

3 1/2 cups milk

1/2 cup water

1 cup chopped watercress or arugula

1 cup chopped romaine lettuce

1/2 cup chopped flat leaf parsley

1/2 cup finely shredded carrot

In a medium saucepan, melt butter or margarine over medium heat; stir in flour, salt, and turmeric and stir constantly until bubbly, about one minute. Gradually stir in milk and cook, stirring constantly until smooth and slightly thickened. In another pan, bring water to a boil and add greens and carrots; stir briefly then add (undrained) to milk mixture. Heat just to boiling.

Makes 8 servings

Gather bell peppers of every color—purple, red, green, yellow, and orange—place them in a wicker basket and use as a centerpiece for a special brunch. Next day, slice and sauté the peppers with onions and garlic to top an omelet or pasta.

BLACK BEAN CHILI

2 tablespoons vegetable oil
1 onion, chopped
1 clove garlic, minced or mashed
1 green pepper, seeded and chopped
3 (15-ounce) cans black beans, drained and rinsed
1 (15-ounce) can chopped tomatoes (do not drain)
1 (15-ounce) can corn, drained
1 teaspoon chili powder
1 teaspoon ground cumin
1/2 teaspoon oregano
1/2 teaspoon red pepper sauce, or to taste
1 teaspoon salt

In a large saucepan, heat oil over medium heat. Stir in onion and garlic; sauté until onion is clear; add green pepper and sauté until pepper is soft. Stir in remaining ingredients and bring to a boil. Reduce heat and simmer, uncovered, for 20 minutes or until thick.

Makes 8 servings

When you have only dried herbs and would like to refresh them to use in a favorite recipe, try chopping the dried herb together with fresh parsley. The parsley will moisten the herb and revitalize its flavor while adding its own freshness to your dish.

TOMATOES STUFFED WITH PESTO RICE

8 large ripe tomatoes
2 tablespoons olive oil
1 zucchini, grated
1/2 cup chopped onion
2 cloves garlic, minced or mashed
2 cups cooked white or brown rice
1/4 cup chopped fresh basil, or 2 tablespoons dried basil
1/4 cup freshly grated Parmesan cheese
2 tablespoons Dijon mustard
2 tablespoons olive oil
2 tablespoons white wine vinegar
small basil leaves for garnish (optional)

Cut the tops off the tomatoes and with a spoon or your fingers, remove the seeds. If necessary, cut a sliver off the bottoms to make the tomatoes stand up without rolling. Turn them stem side down to drain.

In a large skillet over medium heat, heat oil and add zucchini, onion, and garlic; sauté until the onion is clear and the zucchini is tender. Stir in rice, basil, and cheese. Cook, stirring, just until cheese begins to melt. Remove from heat. In a bowl, whisk together mustard, olive oil, and vinegar. Add mustard mixture to rice mixture and toss. Turn tomatoes over and fill each with about 1/4 cup rice mixture, heaping the rice on top. Garnish with basil leaves, if desired.

Makes 8 servings

OVER-STUFFED BAKED POTATOES

6 large Idaho potatoes, baked
1/2 cup milk
1 cup whipped cottage cheese or ricotta cheese
1 clove garlic, minced or mashed
1/2 teaspoon salt
2 cups cooked, chopped vegetables
(left-over carrots, spinach, broccoli, and/or green beans are good)
1/2 cup grated cheese of any kind

Heat oven to 350° F. Cut the crosswise tops off the potatoes and discard the tops. With a spoon, gently scoop out the flesh of the potatoes leaving "walls" about 1/4-inch thick; put the flesh in a bowl, reserving the skins. Mash the potato flesh with milk; add cottage or ricotta cheese, garlic and salt; mash well. Stir in vegetables and half the cheese. Spoon the potato mixture into the skins, piling it on top; sprinkle with remaining cheese. Place the filled potatoes in a baking dish and bake for 20 minutes or until the tops are lightly brown.

Makes 6 servings

FLAVORED VINEGARS

Vinegars infused with herbs, fruit, or vegetables from the garden are wonderful flavor boosters for salad dressings, marinades, and hot or cold sauces. The process is easy and the results are beautiful and tasty.

First, sterilize bottles or jars by placing them in a large pan and covering with cold water. Bring the water to a slow boil; cover the pan and reduce the heat; simmer for 10 minutes. Remove the bottles with tongs and invert on clean kitchen towels.

Be sure to use fresh vinegar with a 4% to 6% acid content. Never dilute vinegar with water before adding flavoring agents. Clear white vinegar allows the flavor of the infusion to shine through, but you can try red or white wine vinegars as well. Use your vinegar within a year as the flavor dissipates over time.

FRUIT VINEGARS:
Place 1 cup of ripe, fresh raspberries, strawberries, gooseberries, or blackberries in a bottle or jar. Other fruits you can use include pears, cherries, peaches, prunes, apricots, dates, or the zest of any citrus fruit such as orange, lemon, lime, or grapefruit. Add 4 cups vinegar and, if you like a sweet vinegar, add 1/3 cup white sugar or 1/4 cup honey to the bottle. Let steep at room temperature for at least two weeks. Use your vinegar straight from the bottle or strain into another jar or bottle before using.

FRESH HERB VINEGARS:

In the summer, when herbs are plentiful, gather some for making vinegars that will capture a bit of summer's aroma and flavor. Basil— whether red, green, lemon, cinnamon, or opal—is a good choice. Also consider thyme, rosemary, chives, bay leaves, tarragon, parsley, cilantro, watercress, lemon grass, and dill. Leave for two weeks, then strain the vinegar and discard the herbs. You can add a sprig of fresh herb to the vinegar if you like how it looks.

VEGETABLE VINEGARS:

A bonus of adding vegetables to flavor vinegar is that you also get a pickled vegetable to use in salads, pasta sauces, or gravies. Wash the vegetables well, put them in a jar, crock, or bottle, then cover with vinegar. For some vegetables, such as baby carrots, celery hearts, scallions, fennel, bell peppers, or asparagus, fill the jar with the vegetable before adding the vinegar; leave for two weeks then remove the pickled vegetables to be used in other recipes—their flavor will be sharp and the vinegar will retain a whiff of the vegetable. When using onions, garlic, or shallots to flavor vinegar, a little goes a long way. Three cloves of garlic or shallot, or five scallions will adequately flavor 4 cups of vinegar. To get a very concentrated flavor, use more onions and plan to use the intensely flavored vinegar very sparingly.

You can mix herbs, citrus zests, and vegetables in any combination you like. Mint/lemon, honey/garlic, carrot/chive, parsley/lime are a few possibilities. Try adding whole spices, too, including allspice, cinnamon, cloves, dried hot peppers, black peppercorns, or caraway seeds.

CHAPTER TWO

PRIDE OF THE FARM

*L*ucky the cook who can walk out her kitchen door and collect fresh eggs, milk and cheese. Even those who rely on supermarket dairy cases are privileged to choose from a huge variety of dairy products, from fresh, wholesome milk to yogurt, creamy cheeses and flavorful butters.

Family-owned dairy farms continue to be the source of most of the milk products we enjoy today. Growing feed, breeding stock and keeping a farm clean and productive are full-time, year round jobs for dedicated farm families. Much of the milk produced in America is processed into a variety of cheeses, including some that rival the best of European cheese. Today's home cooks and professional chefs alike create beautiful and nutritious dishes based on milk products, especially cheese.

Eggs, too, are the basis for many wonderful meals throughout the day and throughout the year. You can make a perfect omelet or poached eggs to be enjoyed by your family or guests for breakfast, brunch or a late supper.

In addition to protein-packed entrees featuring dairy and egg products, this chapter submits poultry and meat dishes that hale from all regions of America and with various ethnic scents and flavors. Turkey and chicken dishes are among the favorites for many Americans today and with their relatively mild flavor, they readily take to other ingredients that make them exciting entrees. Beef, pork and lamb also make up an important part of our diets and are versatile ingredients in many ethnic American recipes. Experiment, indulge and enjoy the incredible array of possibilities that America's bounty offers.

EGGS:

To Aunt Irene the Ten Commandments seemed almost insignificant compared with the astonishing miracle of what you could do with an egg. As the angel had left in his fiery chariot he must have added, 'And don't forget omelettes, and cake and custard and souffles and poaching and frying and boiling and baking. Oh, and they're frightfully good with anchovies, and you can use the shells to clarify soup—and don't forget to dig them in round the roots of your roses', the angelic tones fading into the ethereal distance.

ALICE THOMAS ELLIS

CHIVE-CREAM CHEESE DINNER OMELET

SAUCE:
6 dried tomato halves
1 tablespoon vegetable oil
1 tablespoon butter or margarine
1 cup half-and-half
1/4 cup water or chicken broth
1 tablespoon chopped parsley

OMELET:
1 package (3 ounces) cream cheese with chives
2 tablespoons water
6 large eggs
1/2 teaspoon salt
1/4 teaspoon pepper

Prepare the sauce: Pour boiling water over dried tomatoes; set aside for 2 minutes to soften. Drain tomatoes and cut into slivers. In a skillet, heat oil and butter or margarine together over medium heat; stir in half-and-half and chicken broth and simmer 2 minutes or until beginning to thicken. Whisk in dried tomatoes and parsley; remove from heat, cover, and set aside.

Prepare the omelets: In a large bowl, mash cream cheese; gradually add water until smooth. Beat in eggs, one at a time, add salt and pepper; beat until foamy. Heat an omelet pan or 8-inch skillet over medium-high heat; add a little butter and heat until it stops bubbling. For each omelet, pour 1/3 cup egg mixture into hot butter. With a spatula, gently lift the edges of the omelet as it sets to allow the uncooked egg to run underneath. Continue until the top of the omelet is set but very soft. Lift half the omelet and flip it in half, then onto a warm serving plate. Repeat until all the egg mixture is used. Divide sauce evenly among the omelets and serve.
Makes 6 servings

PASTA OMELET WITH ONIONS, PEPPERS, AND HAM

2 tablespoons olive oil
1 medium onion, sliced into rounds
1/2 cup chopped bell pepper, red, yellow, or green
3 green onions, chopped, including some green
1/2 cup chopped ham, or 4 slices bacon, cooked and crumbled
1/2 teaspoon salt
1/2 teaspoon dried oregano
1 cup cooked pasta of any shape
6 large eggs, lightly beaten
1/4 cup grated Parmesan cheese

In a large skillet, heat oil over medium-high heat. Add onion, pepper, and scallions; sauté until the onion is clear and the pepper soft. Remove from heat; stir in ham, salt, oregano, and pasta. Return to heat and pour eggs over all, turning skillet to let eggs go to bottom. As bottom sets, lift the edges of the omelet with a spatula to allow eggs to run underneath. When the top is set but very soft, sprinkle with cheese. Place under a broiler or in 500° F oven to melt and lightly brown the cheese. Cut into wedges to serve.
Makes 4 to 6 servings

HERBED EGG SALAD

5 eggs, hard cooked, peeled, and minced
1/3 cup melted butter or margarine
1 tablespoon white wine vinegar
1 tablespoon minced fresh dill
1 tablespoon minced fresh parsley
1 tablespoon minced fresh chives
1 teaspoon mustard
1/2 teaspoon salt
2 dashes red hot pepper sauce

In a medium bowl, mix all the ingredients together until well blended. Use as a sandwich spread or as a dip for cut vegetables.
Makes about 2 cups

"DROPPED" EGGS ON TOAST

1 teaspoon vinegar
1/2 teaspoon salt
4 large eggs
4 slices whole wheat bread or English muffin halves
1 1/2 tablespoons butter or margarine

"Dropped"
Eggs on Toast

Fill a large skillet with water to about 1 1/2 inches deep. Bring to a simmer and add vinegar and salt. Remove skillet from heat; one at a time, break the eggs and drop them into the hot water; let stand 3 to 5 minutes or until the whites are set. Meanwhile toast the bread or muffin halves and butter generously. Remove eggs from water with a

skimmer or slotted spoon and drain well; place an egg on each piece of toast.

If you like, you can top eggs with warm marinara sauce or white sauce with chunks of chicken, ham, or shrimp in it; or place a slice of American cheese on each egg, then broil to melt the cheese.

Makes 4 servings

ONION TART WITH GOAT CHEESE

CRUST:
1 cup warm water
1 package dry yeast
2 1/2 cups flour
1 teaspoon salt
1 teaspoon sugar

FILLING:
1 pound (about 5) medium onions
2 tablespoons olive oil
2 cloves garlic
1 teaspoon dry thyme leaves
2 tomatoes
8 ounces goat cheese

Prepare the crust (or use frozen bread dough): Pour the water into a large bowl and sprinkle the yeast, 1 cup of the flour, and the sugar over the water; stir and set aside 5 minutes. Add the salt and stir in the remaining flour, a little at a time until too stiff to stir, then turn out of the bowl and onto a floured surface. Knead until smooth and elastic or about 10 minutes. Return to the bowl, cover and let rise in a warm place until double in bulk, about 1 hour. Punch the dough down with your fist, cover, and let rise again until doubled.

Prepare the filling: Peel and slice the onions into thin rounds. Heat the oil in a large skillet over medium heat; add the onions. Peel and thinly slice the garlic, then add it to the onions, along with the thyme. Cover and cook about 20 minutes, stirring occasionally, until the onions are golden. Peel and remove the seeds from the tomatoes, then chop

them. Stir the tomatoes into the cooked onions, turn up the heat and cook, stirring, until the mixture thickens. Set aside to cool slightly. Heat the oven to 450° F.

Meanwhile, roll out the crust dough to an 11-x 7-inch rectangle, then transfer to an oiled baking sheet. Let the dough rest 10 minutes, then spread the onion mixture over the crust. If the goat cheese is very soft, dab spoonsful over the onion filling; if the cheese is firm, cut it into slices and arrange them on the filling. Let rest for 10 minutes. Bake for 15 to 20 minutes, or until the bottom of the crust is crisp. Cut into 6 or 8 rectangles.

Makes 4 servings

BAKED PANCAKE WITH SWEETENED SOUR CREAM AND BERRIES

PANCAKES:
3 eggs
1/2 cup milk
1/2 cup flour
pinch of salt
2 tablespoons melted butter

TOPPING:
2/3 cup sour cream
2 tablespoons sugar
1 cup berries (sliced strawberries, blueberries, etc.)

Heat oven to 450° F.

Make the pancakes: In a mixing bowl, whisk the eggs and milk together until light and fluffy. Whisk in the flour and salt until well blended, then add the butter and blend until smooth. Lightly grease two 6-inch cake pans; pour batter in the pans. Bake for 15 minutes.

Make the topping: In a small bowl, mix the sour cream and sugar together; set aside so sugar has time to melt.

Serve the pancakes immediately from the oven topped with sour cream, sugar, and berries.

Makes 2 servings

. . . I have cooked dinner every night this week. I am inclined to put in far too much flavoring, as in painting I put far too much color, but I am learning restraint. I am also learning to be fearless with eggs and undismayed by deep fat and flour and bread crumbs. It all comes under the heading of living dangerously. . .

NOEL COWARD

DAIRY:

COOL BUTTERMILK SOUP

4 tablespoons butter or margarine
2 onions, peeled and chopped
3 cucumbers, peeled, seeded, and chopped
1 teaspoon salt
1/8 teaspoon nutmeg
3 cups chicken broth
2 tablespoons flour
1 cup buttermilk
2 tablespoons fresh dill, minced
2 tablespoons fresh chives, minced
whole chives for garnish, optional

In a large skillet, melt 2 tablespoons of the butter or margarine; add onions and cucumbers and sauté 10 minutes, until onions are golden. Stir in salt, nutmeg, and chicken broth; cover and simmer 15 minutes. Remove from heat and let cool slightly, then purée in a blender or food processor. (Caution: Never process boiling liquid!) In a large pan, melt 2 tablespoons of butter and blend in flour and stir until bubbly. Add cucumber purée and heat, stirring constantly, until thickened. Remove from heat and stir in buttermilk, dill, and chives. Serve chilled garnished with whole chives, if desired.

Makes 4 to 6 servings

Southern Cheese Grits

WISCONSIN CHEESE FONDUE

1 clove garlic
2 tablespoons butter or margarine
2 cups grated sharp Wisconsin Cheddar or Colby cheese
1 tablespoon flour
1/3 cup beer
1 small loaf Italian or French bread

Rub inside of a double boiler with cut clove of garlic; set over simmering water. Add butter and let melt. Put the cheese in a bowl, sprinkle with flour, and toss together. Add the cheese and beer to the butter, then mix rapidly until the cheese is melted. Pour into a fondue pot or chafing dish and serve immediately with chunks of bread and long forks.

Makes 2 to 4 servings

SOUTHERN CHEESE GRITS

1 cup quick-cooking grits
1 teaspoon salt
4 cups water
1 1/2 cups (about 6 ounces) smooth process cheese, cut into chunks
1/2 cup milk
2 eggs, lightly beaten
1/2 cup (about 2 ounces) Cheddar cheese, grated

Heat oven to 350° F. Cook grits in salted water according to package directions. Add process cheese and stir until melts. Stir in milk and eggs. Pour into greased 1 1/2- or 2-quart shallow casserole and bake 40 minutes; remove from oven, sprinkle with Cheddar cheese, and bake another 5 minutes.

Makes 8 to 10 servings

Cheese is milk that has grown up. . . . It is preeminently the food of man—the older it grows the more manly it becomes, and in the last stages of senility it almost requires a room to itself . . . .

EDWARD BUNYARD

SHAKER-STYLE RAREBIT

4 cups (about 8 ounces)
shredded Cheddar cheese

2 cups whole milk or
light cream

1/2 teaspoon nutmeg

8 slices toast

Mix the cheese and milk
together in a large pan; stir
over medium heat until
smooth and hot. Stir in nutmeg. Serve over toast.

Makes 4 servings

Shaker-Style Rarebit

CITY
SOUFFLÉ

6 slices bread, cubed
4 eggs
2 cups milk
1 teaspoon dry mustard
1 teaspoon salt
4 cups (about 8 ounces) grated cheese of any kind

Place bread cubes in a greased 1 1/2-quart shallow casserole. In a large bowl, beat together eggs, milk, dry mustard, salt, and cheese; pour over the bread, cover, and refrigerate at least one hour or overnight. Heat oven to 350° F. Place casserole in a larger pan and add boiling water to an inch deep; bake one hour or until puffed and golden.

If you like, add 1 cup chopped cooked ham; 6 slices crisp, crumbled bacon; or 1 small onion, chopped and sautéed until golden.

Makes 4 to 6 servings

HERBED
CHEESE SPREADS

Cheese spreads keep well and are versatile—keep some in the refrigerator to serve with a basket of crackers for parties or after-school snacks. Or thin any of these spreads with milk and serve with fresh cut vegetables. And cheese spreads also melt nicely over hot baked potatoes or other vegetables or pasta.

Begin with 8 ounces of cream cheese and add any of the following:

• 2 cups grated Cheddar cheese with 1 teaspoon red hot pepper sauce, 1 tablespoon finely chopped green onion, and 1 clove garlic, minced

• 1 cup chopped pimento-stuffed green olives and 1 teaspoon dry oregano

• 1 (4-ounce) can deviled ham and 1 tablespoon prepared brown mustard

• 1/2 cup crumbled blue cheese, 1 tablespoon mayonnaise, 1 tablespoon lemon juice, and 1 teaspoon dill seed

• 1/2 cup milk, 1 tablespoon prepared horseradish, and 1/2 cup crisp, crumbled bacon

• 1/2 cup sour cream, 1/4 cup grated Parmesan cheese, and 1/2 teaspoon dry Italian seasoning

• 1/4 cup milk and 1/4 cup minced fresh chives

• 2 tablespoons mayonnaise, 1 tablespoon lemon juice, 1 (2-ounce) jar pimentos, diced with juice, and 1/4 teaspoon red hot pepper sauce

BLUE CHEESE POTATO CASSEROLE

3 cups cottage cheese
1/2 cup (about 2 ounces) blue cheese, crumbled
4 cups hot unseasoned mashed potatoes
(made from fresh or mix)
1/2 cup sour cream
2 tablespoons finely chopped green onions
1 teaspoon salt

Heat oven to 350° F. Place cottage cheese and blue cheese in a blender or food processor and process until smooth. In a large bowl, mix together the cheeses with potatoes, sour cream, green onions, and salt. Spoon into a greased 2-quart casserole; make peaks on the surface with the back of a spoon. Bake uncovered 30 minutes, until lightly browned.

Makes 6 servings

POULTRY:

TURKEY AND VEGETABLE MEATLOAF

1/4 cup butter or margarine
1/2 cup minced green onion
1/2 cup minced yellow onion
1/2 cup minced celery
1/2 cup minced carrot
1/2 cup minced red or green pepper
2 cloves garlic, minced
1 teaspoon salt
1/2 teaspoon red hot pepper sauce
1/2 teaspoon cumin
1/2 teaspoon nutmeg

1/2 cup milk or water
1/2 cup ketchup
2 pounds ground turkey
3 eggs, lightly beaten
1 cup fresh bread crumbs

Melt butter or margarine in a large skillet and sauté vegetables until soft; set aside and cool to room temperature. Heat oven to 350° F. Stir salt, pepper sauce, cumin, nutmeg, water, and ketchup into vegetables. In a large bowl, lightly mix together vegetables, turkey, eggs, and bread crumbs. Form into a loaf on a large baking pan. Bake 45 minutes.

Makes 6 to 8 servings

Turkey and
Vegetable Meatloaf

SMOTHERED TURKEY BREAST

2 tablespoons vegetable oil
8 slices uncooked turkey breast (about 1 1/4 pounds)
1 large onion, chopped
1 garlic clove, chopped
1 (15-ounce) can chopped tomatoes, drained and juice reserved
1/4 cup fresh parsley, chopped
1 teaspoon dried rosemary, crushed
1 bay leaf
1 teaspoon salt
about 1/2 cup reserved tomato juice

Heat oil in a large skillet over medium-high heat. Brown turkey slices lightly in the oil. Remove turkey from the pan and reserve. Sauté onion and garlic in the drippings in the skillet. When onions are golden, add the turkey, tomatoes, parsley, rosemary, bay leaf, and salt. Bring to a boil, reduce heat, and simmer 20 minutes, adding reserved tomato juice as needed if sauce becomes too thick. Remove bay leaf before serving over hot noodles.

Makes 4 servings

TURKEY CUTLETS
WITH GRAPEFRUIT SAUCE

1 cup grapefruit juice
2 cups sweet white wine or chicken stock
2 carrots, chopped
2 stalks celery, chopped
6 peppercorns
1 bay leaf
8 slices turkey breast (about 1 1/4 pounds)
chopped parsley and grated grapefruit peel for garnish

Pour grapefruit juice and wine or stock into a large skillet; add carrots, celery, peppercorns, and bay leaf; bring to a boil, reduce heat and simmer for 10 minutes. Add turkey breast and poach gently for 8 minutes, or until turkey is no longer pink inside. Remove turkey, carrots, and celery and arrange on serving platter. Garnish with parsley and grapefruit peel if desired.

Makes 4 servings

Turkey Cutlets with Grapefruit Sauce

BUTTERMILK FRIED CHICKEN

1 frying chicken, cut into serving pieces and
skin removed
2 cups buttermilk
2/3 cup flour
1 teaspoon salt
1/2 teaspoon baking powder
1/4 teaspoon pepper
1/4 teaspoon paprika
1/4 teaspoon garlic powder, optional
vegetable oil or shortening

Place the chicken pieces in a shallow pan in one layer, then cover with buttermilk; cover and refrigerate for 1 to 3 hours, turning occasionally. In a paper bag, shake together the flour, salt, baking powder, pepper, paprika, and garlic powder, if using. Heat oil or shortening about 1/2-inch deep in a large skillet or electric frying pan to 360° F or until a cube of bread sizzles. While oil heats, remove chicken from buttermilk and let drain, but don't wipe. Discard buttermilk. Shake chicken thoroughly in seasoned flour, one piece at a time, beginning with the meatiest pieces. Place gently in hot oil and fry about 20 minutes on each side, turning only once, until juices from thigh run clear. Drain well on paper towels and serve.

Makes 4 servings

GRILLED CHICKEN KEBABS

1/2 cup soy sauce

1/4 cup sherry or orange juice

1/2 teaspoon liquid smoke

1 teaspoon brown sugar

2 teaspoons finely grated fresh ginger or

1 teaspoon powdered ginger

2 garlic cloves, halved

3 whole, skinned, and boned chicken breasts

16 mushrooms

16 green onions, trimmed and cut to 2 inches long
(white part only)

fresh cilantro, chopped for garnish

In a shallow non-aluminum pan, stir together the soy sauce, sherry or juice, liquid smoke, brown sugar, ginger, and garlic. Cut each chicken breast in half, then each half into 8 chunks, so you have 48 pieces. Place the chicken in the soy mixture, cover, and refrigerate 2 hours. Meanwhile, soak 16 (12-inch) bamboo skewers in water to prevent their burning.

Heat oven broiler or prepare outdoor grill. Remove chicken from marinade, reserving marinade. Thread chicken, mushrooms, and onions onto *two parallel skewers* for each serving. Using two skewers will stabilize the food and prevent it from rolling as it's turned during cooking. Alternate chicken with mushrooms and onions, allowing six chicken chunks, two mushrooms, and two onions on each set of two skewers. Broil or grill about 8 minutes, turning frequently and brushing with reserved marinade until chicken is brown and cooked through. (Discard extra marinade—do not serve it as a sauce.) Serve kebabs sprinkled with cilantro over hot rice.

Makes 4 servings

ORANGE-ROSEMARY ROAST CHICKEN

1 (5-pound) roasting chicken
kosher salt
2 thin-skinned juice oranges
10 sprigs fresh rosemary
10 sprigs fresh parsley
24 shallots, peeled
12 garlic cloves, unpeeled
1/2 cup dry white wine or chicken stock

Heat oven to 400° F. Rub inside of chicken with kosher salt and the juice of one orange. Rinse the remaining orange and cut it into 8 wedges. Fill cavity of chicken with orange wedges, half the rosemary, and half the parsley. Truss the chicken with twine and place breast side up in a shallow roasting pan. Roast for 45 minutes, then scatter shallots, garlic, and remaining herbs in pan around chicken, then pour wine or stock over the herbs. Roast another hour or until thigh moves easily and juices run clear. Let rest 10 minutes before carving and serve with the roasted shallots and garlic.

Makes 4 to 6 servings

INDIVIDUAL CHICKEN POT PIES

1/4 cup butter or margarine
1/3 cup flour
1 cup milk
2 cups chicken stock or dry white wine
3 cups chopped cooked chicken
1 tablespoon fresh parsley, chopped
1 teaspoon salt
1/2 teaspoon dried sage
1/2 teaspoon dried thyme
2 cups cooked carrots, sliced or chopped
2 cups cooked green peas
2 (9-inch) refrigerated pie crusts, unbaked
1 egg yolk mixed with 1 tablespoon water

Orange-Rosemary Roast Chicken

Heat oven to 425° F. In a large saucepan, melt the butter or margarine and blend in the flour. Cook and stir over medium heat until flour is bubbly, then stir in milk and stock or wine until thickened. Add chicken, parsley, salt, sage, and thyme; let simmer 5 minutes. Stir in carrots and peas. Divide chicken mixture among 8 (12-ounce) ceramic or disposable pans; set aside. Roll out pie crusts, one at a time, and cut with cookie cutters or with a knife and place on casseroles. Brush each pastry with the egg yolk mixture. Bake 30 to 40 minutes, or until brown and bubbly.

Makes 8 servings

HUNTER STYLE CHICKEN

1 cup flour
1 teaspoon salt
1/4 teaspoon pepper
1 frying chicken, cut into serving pieces with skin removed
2 tablespoons olive or vegetable oil
2 tablespoons butter or margarine
1 large onion, sliced into thin rings
1 cup sliced fresh mushrooms
1/2 cup finely minced ham or 4 strips crisp bacon,
crumbled (optional)
2 tablespoons fresh parsley, chopped
1 (16-ounce) can tomato wedges, not drained
1/2 teaspoon cinnamon
1/4 teaspoon cloves
1/4 cup packed brown sugar
1 cup dry sherry or red wine
1/2 cup slivered almonds

In a paper bag, shake together the flour, salt, and pepper. Put the chicken in the bag, one piece at a time, and shake to coat the chicken. In a large skillet, heat the oil with the butter or margarine. Brown the chicken then remove it to a shallow 3-quart baking dish. Heat the oven to 375° F. In the same skillet, cook the onion rings until transparent. Add the mushrooms, ham or bacon (if using), parsley, tomatoes with liquid, cinnamon, cloves, sherry or wine, and brown sugar; simmer uncovered for 15 minutes. Pour the tomato mixture over the chicken and sprinkle with almonds. Bake 30 to 40 minutes or until chicken is done.

Makes 4 servings

ABOVE
AND RIGHT:
Chicken Chorizo

CHICKEN CHORIZO

SAUCE:

1 (8-ounce) can tomato sauce

1 teaspoon ground cumin

1 teaspoon chili powder

1/2 teaspoon ground coriander

CHICKEN:

1/2 cup fine dry bread crumbs

1 tablespoon chili powder

1/2 teaspoon ground cumin

4 chicken breast halves, skinned and boned

1 (4-ounce) can chopped green chilies, drained

1/4 pound bulk Chorizo sausage, cooked and drained

1/3 cup butter or margarine, melted

chopped green onion for garnish

Prepare the sauce: Combine tomato sauce, cumin, chili powder, and coriander in a small saucepan; heat to boiling and set aside.

Prepare the chicken: On a plate, mix together the bread crumbs, chili powder, and cumin; set aside. Pound chicken breasts until thin. Spread chilies and sausage on chicken and roll up jelly-roll fashion and secure with toothpicks. Dip each chicken breast in melted butter then roll in bread crumb mixture. Place chicken in baking dish, cover, and refrigerate at least one hour. Heat oven to 400° F. Bake chicken 30 minutes. Meanwhile, reheat sauce and pour over chicken before serving. Garnish with green onion.

Makes 4 servings

COUNTRY CAPTAIN CHICKEN

1 (5-pound) roasting or stewing hen

2 stalks celery

2 bay leaves

3 tablespoons olive or vegetable oil

2 onions, chopped

1 clove garlic, chopped

2 green bell peppers, cored, seeded, and chopped

2 (29-ounce) cans tomatoes, undrained

1 tablespoon curry powder

2 teaspoons salt

1 teaspoon dried thyme

1 teaspoon cayenne pepper

1/4 teaspoon cloves

3 cups reserved chicken stock

1/2 cup currants

Place chicken and giblets in a large Dutch oven with celery and bay leaves; pour 2 quarts of water into pan; simmer 1 1/2 to 2 hours or until chicken is very tender. Remove chicken from stock; set chicken aside until cool enough to pull meat from the bones. Strain the stock and reserve 3 cups. (Refrigerate or freeze remaining stock for another use.) In the same pan, heat the oil, then sauté the onion, garlic, and green peppers 10 minutes or until soft. Add tomatoes, curry powder, salt, cayenne, thyme, cloves, reserved stock, and currants and simmer uncovered 45 minutes. Meanwhile, skin chicken and remove meat from bones and cut chicken and giblets into bite-size pieces. Add chicken to sauce and simmer another 15 minutes. Serve over hot rice.

Makes 8 servings

BEEF, LAMB, AND PORK:

HOT BEEFY CHILI

1 pound bacon, cut into 1/2 inch pieces

4 pounds round steak, cut into 1/2 inch cubes

2 (29-ounce) cans tomatoes, undrained

1 (15-ounce) can tomato sauce

1 (6-ounce) can tomato paste

1 (7-ounce) can chopped green chilies, drained

1 jalapeño pepper, seeded and diced

2 large onions, chopped

2 green bell peppers, cored, seeded, and chopped

1 cup fresh parsley, chopped

3 cloves garlic, minced

2 tablespoons ground cumin

2 tablespoons chili powder

1 tablespoon lemon juice

2 teaspoons ground coriander

2 teaspoons salt

1 teaspoon black pepper

1 teaspoon cayenne pepper

1 teaspoon dried oregano

1/2 teaspoon cinnamon

4 (16-ounce) cans pinto beans, drained and rinsed

sour cream and shredded cheese for garnish

In a large skillet, brown bacon; remove from skillet and reserve bacon grease. In same skillet, brown round steak, then put the round steak and bacon in a large stock pot. Add the tomatoes with liquid, tomato sauce, tomato paste, green chilies, and jalapeño to beef and bacon in stock pot; simmer uncovered. Meanwhile, in the skillet heat 2 tablespoons reserved bacon grease and sauté onions until transparent then add to stock pot; sauté green peppers in 2 tablespoons reserved bacon grease until soft then add to stock pot. Add to stock pot: parsley, garlic, ground cumin, chili powder, lemon juice, ground coriander, salt, black pepper, cayenne pepper, oregano, and cinnamon; stir well and simmer uncovered 4 hours, stirring occasionally. Add pinto beans and simmer another 30 minutes. Serve immediately or refrigerate overnight before serving garnished with sour cream and cheese.

Makes 10 to 12 servings

BARBECUED HAMBURGERS

1 pound lean ground beef
2 tablespoons chili sauce
1 tablespoon red wine vinegar
1 teaspoon chili powder
1/8 teaspoon cayenne pepper

Place cold ground beef in a bowl and with a wooden spoon, mix in remaining ingredients. Shape beef into 4 patties, then refrigerate. Meanwhile, heat broiler or prepare outdoor grill. Broil or grill patties 4 inches from heat, about 6 minutes per side for medium, turning only once.

DORMITORY-STYLE "SHEPHERD'S PIE"

FILLING:
1 tablespoon olive or vegetable oil
1 onion, chopped
1 pound lean ground beef
1 tablespoon chili powder
1/2 teaspoon salt
1/2 teaspoon dried oregano
1/2 teaspoon ground cumin
1 (8-ounce) can tomato sauce
1 cup cooked vegetables
(peas, carrots, corn, beans, or mixed)
2 cups (about 8 ounces) shredded Cheddar or
Monterey jack cheese

CRUST:
3/4 cup cornmeal
1/4 cup flour
2 teaspoons baking powder
1 teaspoon salt
1 cup milk
1 egg

Heat oven to 400° F. Prepare the filling: In a large skillet, heat the oil, then sauté the onion until transparent; add ground beef and cook until brown. Drain any fat. Stir in chili powder, oregano, salt, and cumin; heat, stirring, until sizzling; remove from heat and stir in tomato sauce and vegetables. Pour beef mixture into a 9- x 13-inch baking dish; sprinkle with cheese and set aside.

Prepare the crust: In a medium bowl, stir together the cornmeal, flour, baking powder, and salt. In a large measuring cup, lightly beat the milk and egg together then pour into dry ingredients. Stir just until well blended; do not over mix. Spread the thick batter over the cheese-topped beef mixture. Bake 30 minutes or until crust is brown and filling is bubbly.

Makes 6 to 8 servings

Dormitory-Style "Shepherd's Pie"

ONION-CHUTNEY FLANK STEAK

1 (8-ounce) jar mango chutney, finely chopped
1/2 cup tarragon white wine vinegar
1 small onion, finely chopped
1 (3-pound) flank steak

In a shallow non-aluminum baking dish, mix the chutney, vinegar, and onion. Score the flank steak with a small sharp knife in a crisscross pattern about 1/4 inch deep and 1 inch apart. Turn the steak in the marinade, cover, and refrigerate 4 to 6 hours, turning occasionally. Remove from refrigerator and allow to come to room temperature, about an hour. Heat the broiler or prepare outdoor grill. Broil 3 inches from heat about 4 minutes per side. (Flank steak should be served rare.) Carve on a board that will catch juices and cut on the diagonal into slices about 1/4-inch thick.

Makes 6 servings

BOSTON LAMB STEW

5 medium potatoes, peeled and quartered
2 pounds neck of lamb or lamb stew meat
3 onions, sliced into thin rings
6 carrots, cut into 1-inch chunks
1 tablespoon salt
4 cups water
fresh parsley, chopped, for garnish

Begin early in the day or the day before serving. In a large Dutch oven, layer half the potatoes, all the lamb, onions, and carrots, then the remaining potatoes. Add salt and water; cover tightly and simmer 2 hours. Allow to cool, then refrigerate for 3 hours or overnight. Remove fat from top of stew, then reheat over low heat. Ladle into bowls and sprinkle with parsley.

Makes 4 to 6 servings

PORK-STUFFED LEG OF LAMB

1 (3 1/2-pound) boned and
butterflied leg of lamb
1/4 cup fresh parsley, chopped
1/4 cup mixed fresh herbs (such as rosemary, sage, thyme, or oregano), chopped
2 cloves garlic, chopped
1/2 teaspoon salt
2 tablespoons vegetable oil
1 (1-pound) pork tenderloin
1 cup beef stock
1 tablespoon cornstarch

Heat oven to 325° F. Untie and spread lamb on clean work surface. In a small bowl, mix the parsley, herbs, garlic, salt, and oil to make a paste; spread herb mixture onto lamb. Place pork loin on center of lamb and roll it up; tie securely with kitchen twine. Insert a meat thermometer through lamb and into pork. Place roast on a rack in a roasting pan and bake 2 1/2 to 3 hours or until the thermometer reads 170° F. Remove roast to a warm platter and keep warm. Skim fat from surface of pan drippings; scrape up any brown bits. Place the roasting pan over low heat on top of the stove; stir beef stock and cornstarch together, then add to the drippings, stirring constantly until thickened. Simmer 2 minutes. Slice roast and serve with sauce.

Makes 8 to 10 servings

When you have left-over poultry or meat in the refrigerator, you have a feast at hand! Create over-stuffed sandwiches with very thin slices of turkey and fresh apples layered with arugula on buttered pumpernickel bread. Or try a sandwich of cold beef or pork with slices of red onion spread with country mustard on rye bread. When only bits of meat remain on the bone, scrape it clean and use the meat in pasta sauce, then simmer the bones with root vegetables to make a soup stock.

Onion-Chutney Flank Steak

WINTER TIME BEEF STEW

2 pounds lean beef stew meat, cut into
bite-size pieces
1 envelope dry onion soup mix
8 large red potatoes, unpeeled, cut
into quarters
8 carrots, cut into 1-inch pieces
12 mushrooms, quartered
3 celery stalks, cut into 1-inch pieces
3 onions, quartered
2 (8-ounce) cans tomato sauce
1/2 cup dry red wine or beef stock

In a Dutch oven or casserole with a
tight-fitting lid, place beef and sprinkle with dry onion soup mix. Add
vegetables, tomato sauce, and wine or
stock. Cover and bake at 250° F for
5 hours.
    Makes 8 to 10 servings

Winter Time Beef Stew

PERFECT POT ROAST

2 tablespoons vegetable oil
1 (4- to 5-pound) boned, rolled, and tied rump or chuck roast
2 onions, sliced into rings
2 teaspoons salt
1/4 cup cold water
2 cups beef stock or water
1 cup dry red wine or additional beef stock
2/3 cup flour

Heat oil in a large Dutch oven with a tight fitting lid. Brown beef on all sides over medium heat. Add onions as beef browns and allow onions to get very dark brown, which will add color and flavor to the sauce. Add salt and cold water to beef; cover tightly and bring to simmer. Do not allow to boil. Cover tightly and simmer 3 hours, checking frequently and adding 1 or 2 tablespoons water only if needed. Remove beef to a heated platter and keep warm.

Pour off all but 2 tablespoons fat from drippings in Dutch oven. Add 2 cups stock or water to pan and heat, stirring up any brown bits. Gradually add red wine to flour, stirring until smooth, then slowly pour wine mixture into pan, stirring until thick and bubbly. Let simmer for 2 or 3 minutes. Check for seasonings and add more salt if needed. Cut pot roast into 1/2-inch slices and serve with the sauce.

Makes 6 to 8 servings

MARINATED & SKEWERED PORK

MARINADE:
1/2 cup ginger ale
1 tablespoon frozen orange juice concentrate (undiluted)
1 tablespoon olive oil

1 tablespoon lemon juice
1 clove garlic, peeled and crushed
1 1/2 pounds boned pork loin, trimmed of fat and cut into 1/4-inch slices about 1 x 3 inches

SKEWERS:
2 Granny Smith apples, peeled, cored, and cut into 1/2-inch cubes

Prepare the marinade: In a non-aluminum shallow baking dish, stir together the ginger ale, orange juice, oil, lemon juice, and garlic. Count the number of pork strips you cut and soak half that number of 12-inch bamboo skewers in water so they don't burn during cooking. Turn the pork strips in the marinade, cover, and refrigerate 4 to 6 hours, turning occasionally. Heat the broiler or prepare outdoor grill.

Prepare the skewers: Thread the pork strips onto skewers (2 strips per skewer), inserting the point of the skewer into each strip 3 times with an apple cube alternating with each insertion. (You'll have 5 apple cubes on each skewer.) Broil or grill 4 inches from heat 8 to 10 minutes or until well browned. Serve over hot rice.

Makes 4 to 6 servings

What is sauce for the goose may be sauce for the gander, but it is not necessarily sauce for the chicken, the duck, the turkey or the guinea hen.

ALICE B. TOKLAS

SAUSAGE BRUNCH CASSEROLE

2 tablespoons butter or margarine
6 slices white or rye bread
1 pound bulk sausage, cooked and drained of fat
1 cup (about 4 ounces) shredded Swiss cheese
3 eggs
1 1/2 cups milk
1/8 teaspoon nutmeg

Heat oven to 350° F. Put the butter or margarine in a 9- x 13-inch baking dish and place in oven until butter melts. Allow to cool slightly, then place bread slices over melted butter. Sprinkle sausage over bread; sprinkle cheese over sausage. In a small bowl, beat together the eggs, milk, and nutmeg; pour over cheese. Bake 30 minutes or until set.

Makes 6 to 8 servings

Perfect Pot Roast

TEXAS-STYLE RIBS

4 pounds spareribs, cut into serving-size pieces

1/3 cup orange juice

1/3 cup lemon juice

1/3 cup ketchup

1/3 cup packed dark brown sugar

1 tablespoon prepared mustard

1 teaspoon horseradish

1/4 teaspoon red hot pepper sauce

RIGHT:

Texas-Style Ribs

Heat oven to 450° F. Place spareribs in a large, non-aluminum baking pan and roast 30 minutes, turning once to render excess fat. Drain off and discard fat from pan. Turn oven off. Mix together orange juice, lemon juice, ketchup, brown sugar, mustard, horseradish, and pepper sauce; pour over ribs, cover and allow to stand at room temperature 1 hour. Heat oven to 325° F. Uncover ribs and bake 1 hour or until brown, basting often with sauce from pan.

Makes 4 servings

CHAPTER THREE

FRESH AND SALT WATER FARE

*T*he very first people who discovered and set-
tled in America thousands of years ago must
have been awed by the abundance and variety of
fish and seafood that crowded America's lakes,
rivers, streams and oceans. Through time, entire
cultures have sustained themselves on the fish
and seafood they captured, cooked and preserved.

Fishing is now one of the favorite sports of
Americans who drop their lines over the sides of
bridges and cabin cruisers. Cleaning and taking
home the day's catch is only part of the rewards
of a quiet, relaxing time spent fishing. And, of
course, throughout the year, fishmongers and mar-
kets offer both locally caught and farmed fish as
well as seafood flown in from distant ports.

Fish farming is a relatively new way of ensuring
a stock of fresh and salt water fish to America's
tables. By controlling the type of feed and the
environment where the fish live, growers supply
fish that is tasty, nutritious and clean. Farms in the
South produce catfish that is sold fresh or frozen,
sometimes in flavorful sauces ready to be baked
or microwaved, while farms in the West grow
salmon and trout that are grilled, baked or broiled.
For the best-tasting fish and seafood, prepare it
according to recipe instructions and be careful to
avoid over-cooking.

From a nutritional aspect, adding fish to your
family's menus is wise; and, the flavor and variety
of fish and seafood is hard to beat. Many fish are
low in fat and high in protein; even those that are
higher in fat supply fatty acids that have proven to
be health enhancing. Try the following recipes
and enjoy the harvest of America's lakes and seas.

SCALLOP AND CABBAGE POT STICKERS

1 cup green cabbage or bok choy, finely chopped
1/2 teaspoon salt
1/2 pound fresh raw scallops, finely chopped
1 tablespoon light soy sauce
1/8 teaspoon sugar
1 teaspoon fresh ginger, finely chopped
1 green onion, finely chopped
1 tablespoon cornstarch dissolved in 1/4 cup water
1 tablespoon sesame oil
24 (3-inch) round or square dumpling wrappers
2 tablespoons vegetable oil
1 cup boiling water

DIPPING SAUCE:
1/4 cup light soy sauce
2 tablespoons red wine vinegar
2 teaspoons fresh ginger, finely shredded
1 teaspoon green onion, finely chopped

Place cabbage in a sieve and sprinkle with 1/2 teaspoon salt; leave 5 minutes then press to remove excess water; pat cabbage with paper towels and set aside. In a bowl, stir together the cabbage, scallops, soy sauce, sugar, ginger, green onion, dissolved cornstarch, and sesame oil; set aside. Keep the dumpling wrappers under a damp towel to prevent their drying and work with one at a time. Hold a wrapper in the palm of one hand and fill with 1 teaspoon filling mixture, then brush the edges of the wrapper with water and fold the wrapper in half. If you like, you can pull the corners of the wrapper together, dampen with water, and squeeze until the corners stick together. As you fill the wrappers, place them under the damp towel.

Heat the vegetable oil in a large skillet with a cover. Place the dumplings in the hot oil and tip the skillet to distribute the oil all around the pan. Add the boiling water, cover, and steam for 2 minutes. Turn heat to low and cook for another 4 minutes. Uncover; turn heat to high to allow any remaining water to evaporate. Let the dumplings sizzle in the remaining oil until golden brown on the bottom. Shake the pan occasionally to prevent dumplings from sticking. Remove to a hot serving platter.

Combine dipping sauce ingredients in a small bowl and serve with the pot stickers.

Makes 4 servings

CLASSIC MARYLAND CRAB CAKES

2 tablespoons butter or margarine
2 tablespoons finely minced onion
2 tablespoons finely minced celery
1 pound fresh crab meat
2 eggs, lightly beaten
2 tablespoons mayonnaise
1 tablespoon Dijon mustard
1 tablespoon fresh parsley, chopped
1/4 teaspoon salt
1/4 teaspoon red hot pepper sauce
2/3 cup fine cracker crumbs
1/4 cup vegetable oil

Melt butter or margarine in a small skillet and sauté onion and celery until the onion is transparent; transfer to a medium mixing bowl. Add the crab meat, eggs, mayonnaise, mustard, parsley, salt, and pepper sauce; mix well. Cover and refrigerate 2 hours. Form mixture into patties 3 inches in diameter and about 1/2-inch thick. Dip each patty in cracker crumbs, coating well. Heat oil in a large skillet over medium high heat and brown both sides of patties, then reduce heat and cook another 5 minutes. Drain well on paper towels and serve with tartar sauce.

Makes 4 servings

For many thousands of years human beings have longed for salt. Until one hundred years ago, salt was to be had only from great distances . . . . Salt has forced man to explore, to think, to work, to travel. To obtain salt he has erected whole political and economic systems; he has fought, built, destroyed, extorted, and haggled.

MARGARET VISSER

Classic Maryland Crab Cakes

NEW ENGLAND STYLE CLAM CHOWDER

3 tablespoons butter or margarine
2 small onions, finely chopped
2 (10-ounce) cans minced clams, drained with
liquid reserved
2 cups peeled potatoes, diced
1 teaspoon salt
2 cups milk
1 cup half-and-half or evaporated milk
chopped green onions and black pepper for garnish

Heat butter or margarine in a saucepan and sauté onion until pale gold. Add liquid from clams, potatoes, and salt; cover and simmer until potatoes are nearly cooked, about 10 minutes. Add clams, milk, and half-and-half, cover and simmer just to heat through, but do not boil. Serve sprinkled with green onions and black pepper.

RIGHT:
Clam Chowder

Makes 6 to 8 servings

SPICY BAY SCALLOPS

1 1/2 pounds bay scallops
1/4 cup butter
1 tablespoon green onion, finely chopped
1 tablespoon fresh parsley, finely chopped
1 tablespoon fresh dill, finely chopped
1/4 cup dry white wine or vermouth
2 tablespoons lemon or lime juice
1/2 teaspoon salt
1/4 teaspoon red hot pepper sauce

Pat scallops with paper towels until dry. Melt the butter in a large skillet over medium-low heat and stir-fry green onion until soft. Add parsley and dill and turn heat up to medium-high, then add scallops and stir-fry until the edges are lightly browned. Remove scallops to a hot platter and keep warm. Add wine or vermouth, lemon or lime juice, salt, and hot pepper sauce to skillet and boil 2 minutes. Pour sauce over scallops; serve with rice.

Makes 4 servings

WINE-STEAMED MUSSELS

1/2 cup butter
1/2 cup onion, finely chopped
3 cloves garlic, chopped
3 dozen mussels in the shell, scrubbed clean
4 sprigs fresh parsley
2 sprigs fresh thyme or 1 teaspoon dried thyme
1 bay leaf
2 cups dry white wine
2 tablespoons fresh parsley, chopped

Melt butter in a large, heavy kettle and sauté onions and garlic until onion is pale gold. Add mussels, parsley sprigs, thyme, bay leaf, and wine, cover and bring to a boil, then reduce heat and simmer 3 minutes until mussels open. Discard unopened mussels. With a slotted spoon, transfer mussels to a serving bowl and keep warm. Strain cooking liquid and return to kettle; add chopped parsley and heat; pour sauce over mussels.

Makes 4 servings

SHRIMP CREOLE

1/4 cup vegetable oil
1 onion, sliced into thin rings
1 cup celery, chopped
1 cup green bell pepper, cut into thin strips
2 (14-ounce) cans chopped tomatoes, undrained
1 (8-ounce) can tomato sauce
2 bay leaves
1 tablespoon sugar
1 tablespoon salt
1 tablespoon chili powder
1/8 teaspoon red hot pepper sauce
2 pounds raw shrimp, peeled
2 tablespoons flour
1/3 cup water

Heat oil in a large skillet over low heat. Sauté onion, celery, and bell pepper until soft but not brown. Add tomatoes, tomato sauce, bay leaves, sugar, salt, chili powder, and pepper sauce. Bring to a boil then reduce heat and simmer 30 minutes. Add shrimp and simmer another 15 minutes. Mix the flour and water together, then add to tomato mixture; cook, stirring, 5 minutes or until thickened. Serve over rice.

Makes 6 to 8 servings

Wine-Steamed Mussels

SHRIMP WITH OKRA, TOMATOES, AND CORN

1/2 pound fresh okra or
1 (10-ounce) package
frozen cut okra
2 tablespoons vegetable oil
1 onion, sliced into thin rings
1 cup niblet corn
1 bell pepper (red or green), cored,
seeded, and chopped
3 large tomatoes, seeded and
chopped
1/2 teaspoon dried thyme
1/2 teaspoon dried oregano
1/2 teaspoon paprika
1/2 teaspoon salt
1/4 teaspoon cayenne
2 pounds raw shrimp, peeled

Trim the ends off okra and cut into 1/4-inch slices, or defrost if frozen. Heat oil in a large skillet. Sauté okra, onion, corn, and bell pepper 5 minutes or until onion is soft. Add tomatoes, thyme, oregano, paprika, salt, cayenne, and shrimp. Cook and stir 5 to 8 minutes or until shrimp is cooked through and vegetables are tender.
   Makes 6 servings

Shrimp with Okra, Tomatoes, and Corn

★ ★ ★ ★ ★ ★ ★ ★ ★ ★ ★ ★   75

CATFISH FRY

2 pounds catfish fillets
flour
2 eggs
1/4 cup water
1/2 cup cornmeal
1/2 cup flour
oil for frying

Sprinkle the fish fillets with salt and pepper then dust with flour. In a shallow bowl, beat eggs with water. In another shallow bowl, stir together cornmeal and flour. In a large skillet, heat oil 1/2-inch deep until it reaches 375° F by a thermometer or until a bread cube browns quickly. Dip floured fish filets in egg, then into cornmeal/flour mixture, then place in hot oil. Fry a few fillets at a time, 5 or 6 minutes, turning as necessary to brown evenly. Keep fried fish hot until all the fillets are done. Drain well on paper towels, then serve with Hush Puppies.

Makes 4 servings

HUSH PUPPIES

2 cups white cornmeal
1 tablespoon flour
1 teaspoon baking soda
1 teaspoon baking powder
1 teaspoon salt
1/3 cup onion, finely chopped
1 egg, lightly beaten
1 cup buttermilk

Heat oil in a deep fat fryer or electric wok to 375° F. Stir together cornmeal, flour, baking soda, baking powder, and salt in a bowl; stir in onion. In a small bowl, stir together the egg and buttermilk; add to dry ingredients and stir lightly only until blended. Drop batter by teaspoons into the hot oil. Cook until golden brown. The hush puppies will float when done. Drain on paper towels and serve hot.

Makes about 40

Catfish Fry

THE LORE AND LURE OF HUSH PUPPIES

Certainly close relations to corn pone, corn bread, corn dodgers, johnny cake, and maybe even corn tortillas, Hush Puppies are a must-serve with fried fish and seafood in the Deep South. Crisp and brown on the outside, soft and flavorful on the inside, they're perfectly bite-size.

Legend has it that Hush Puppies got their colorful name from hunters and fishermen who tossed the cornmeal balls after they cooled to quiet their yapping dogs.

For a typically Southern service, line a large basket with paper or cloth napkins then fill it with hot fried fish and Hush Puppies, and serve with side dishes of tartar sauce, red cocktail sauce, and a bottle of red hot pepper sauce. French fries, batter-fried onion rings, and cole slaw complete the feast.

BAKED SOLE WITH CITRUS FRUIT

1 1/2 pounds fresh or frozen sole fillets, thawed
vegetable oil spray
1 1/2 cups citrus sections, roughly chopped (orange,
blood orange, grapefruit, tangerine, and/or tangelo)
2 tablespoons butter or margarine
1/4 cup onion, finely chopped
1/4 cup orange juice

Heat oven to 400° F. Oil a large, shallow baking dish or spray well with vegetable oil spray. Arrange fish in one layer in dish. In a blender or food processor, process half the citrus sections until smooth and reserve the remainder. In a small skillet, heat butter or margarine then sauté onion until soft; add orange juice and simmer 1 minute. Stir in puréed and reserved citrus; simmer another minute. Pour citrus mixture over sole fillets. Bake 10 minutes or until fish flakes easily with a fork. Serve immediately with rice.

Makes 4 servings

SNAPPER WITH SALSA

1 small onion, cut into thin rings
2 tablespoons water
1 pound red snapper fillets
1 cup mild salsa
1 tomato, seeded and chopped
1/2 cup pitted black olives, sliced
1/2 cup (about 2 ounces) Cheddar or
Monterey jack cheese, finely shredded

Put onion and water in a 7- x 11-inch glass or other microwavable baking dish. Cover with plastic wrap and pierce it with holes. Microwave on high for 3 minutes. Place fish on top of onion, cover again, and microwave for 4 or 5 minutes or until fish flakes easily. Drain off water. Top fish with salsa, tomato, and olives. Cook 2 minutes. Sprinkle with cheese.

Makes 4 servings

MOUNTAIN TROUT ALMONDINE

1/2 cup milk
1 teaspoon salt
4 whole fresh trout, cleaned
1/2 cup fine dry bread crumbs or finely crushed
corn flakes
1/2 cup sliced almonds, finely crushed
4 tablespoons melted butter or margarine

SAUCE:
3/4 cup sliced almonds
1/2 cup butter or margarine
1 tablespoon Worcestershire sauce

Heat oven to 500° F. In a shallow bowl, mix milk and salt. In another shallow bowl, mix bread crumbs or corn flakes and almonds. Dip fish in milk, then roll in crumbs; place in a greased shallow baking dish. Drizzle fish with melted butter or margarine. Bake uncovered, without turning, for 10 to 15 minutes or until fish are crisp and brown.

Meanwhile, make the sauce: In a small skillet, lightly toast almonds, stirring constantly. Add butter or margarine and Worcestershire sauce and heat until butter melts. Pour sauce over fish just before serving, dividing almonds evenly.

Makes 4 servings

Timing is the secret to flavorful, tender fish and seafood. The rule that professional chefs use for cooking fish is: broil, bake, poach or pan fry 10 minutes for each inch of thickness. When you cook fish in a sauce or wrap it in foil or parchment to bake, allow 15 minutes for each inch.

GRILLED ALASKA SALMON WITH BABY VEGETABLES

4 (6- to 8-ounce) salmon steaks
1 pound mixed baby vegetables
(artichokes, carrots, potatoes, squash, or green beans)
1/4 cup light soy sauce
1/4 cup light sesame oil
2 tablespoons fresh lemon juice
1 tablespoon fresh ginger, finely shredded
1/2 teaspoon black pepper
hickory or mesquite chips, soaked in water

Rinse salmon steaks with cold water and pat dry with paper towels. Place fish and vegetables in a shallow baking dish. In a small bowl, stir together the soy sauce, sesame oil, lemon juice, ginger, and pepper. Pour marinade over the fish and vegetables; cover and refrigerate 2 hours or overnight. Remove fish and vegetables from marinade and wrap vegetables loosely in foil. Prepare outdoor grill and scatter wood chips over coals to create smoke. Place foil package on coals and grill salmon on a rack over coals. Grill fish 5 to 8 minutes on each side or until fish flakes easily. Turn foil package with tongs frequently. Unwrap vegetables and serve with the fish.
   Makes 4 servings

SALMON AND ASPARAGUS QUICHE

1 (9-inch) pie crust, unbaked
1 (6-ounce) can salmon, well drained
1/2 pound fresh or frozen asparagus,
cut into 1-inch pieces and lightly steamed
1 cup Swiss cheese, shredded
1 cup milk
2 egg whites
2 eggs
1/2 teaspoon salt
1/4 teaspoon nutmeg

Heat oven to 450° F. Prick pie shell with a fork and bake for 7 minutes; set aside to cool. Reduce oven to 350° F. Sprinkle the crust with salmon, asparagus and cheese. In a bowl, mix together the milk, egg whites, eggs, salt, and nutmeg. Pour carefully over the cheese. Bake 30 minutes or until a knife inserted in the center comes out clean. Cool 5 minutes before cutting.
   Makes 4 to 6 servings

Grilled Alaska Salmon

Top hot fish and seafood

with a flavored butter

you can whip up in a

flash. Begin with a stick

of soft unsalted butter

and add any of the

following:

• *one tablespoon of fine-*
ly chopped fresh herb of
your choice

• *1/4 cup Dijon style or*
country style mustard

• *one tablespoon finely*
grated orange, lime or
lemon zest

• *one tablespoon grated*
red onion and one table-
spoon finely chopped
chives

Form the butter into a

mound and refrigerate

until serving time.

SAN FRANCISCO TUNA STEAKS

4 (6- to 8-ounce) tuna steaks
1 carrot, cut in julienne (matchstick-size) strips
4 green onions, including some green part,
cut in julienne strips
1/4 red bell pepper, cut in julienne strips
2 tablespoons fresh lemon juice or
tarragon flavored white wine vinegar
1 teaspoon salt

Heat oven to 400° F. Brush 4 large squares of foil or parchment paper with vegetable oil or spray with vegetable oil spray. Place tuna steaks on foil or paper. In a bowl, stir together the carrot, green onion, bell pepper, lemon juice, and salt. Place on top of tuna steaks, dividing evenly. Wrap fish and vegetables tightly and place packets on a baking sheet. Bake 30 minutes and check for doneness. If fish doesn't flake easily, rewrap and return to oven for another 5 minutes. Let rest 5 minutes before serving. Place packets on serving plates and cut open at the table.

Makes 4 servings

CITRUS ORANGE ROUGHY

2 pounds orange roughy fillets
1/2 cup fresh lime juice
1/2 cup fresh lemon juice
1/2 cup onion, chopped
2 teaspoons salt
3 tomatoes, seeded and chopped
1/2 cup green onions, chopped
1/4 cup green bell pepper, cored, seeded and chopped
2 tablespoons fresh cilantro, chopped
shredded lettuce
thin strips of lemon and lime zest for garnish

Place fish fillets in the freezer for 10 minutes to firm, but do not allow to freeze. Cut fillets into pieces about 1 1/2-inches square and 1/4-inch thick. In a glass bowl (not metal or plastic) mix together the lime juice, lemon juice, and salt. Gently stir fish into juice mixture; cover and refrigerate overnight. Fish will be white and firm. Drain fish and press gently to remove excess juice. Toss fish lightly with tomatoes, green onions, cilantro, and green pepper. Arrange lettuce on cold salad plates and spoon fish onto lettuce. Garnish with zest strips. (Use halibut or tuna instead of orange roughy, if you prefer.)

Makes 4 servings

CHAPTER FOUR

WILD
WOOD

*M*ost of the products that are so carefully cultivated in gardens and hot houses, as well as the livestock and poultry grown on farms and ranches today were originally found growing and running wild in forests and fields. In the fall, hunters roam hillsides in search of deer, rabbit, and quail, and sometimes harvest wild berries and greens to take home to add to the cooking pot.

Today's well-stocked supermarkets often offer such delicacies as exotic mushrooms, many aromatic fresh herbs, baby greens, sweet berries, farm-raised duck, venison, and rabbit. So, even if we don't have a hunter in the family, we can enjoy the products of the wood and field.

Here you will find some traditional methods and some innovative ways to prepare and serve game and field produce. Rabbit, a long time favorite entree in Europe and Britain, is often overlooked by American cooks, but usually becomes a favorite once it's tried. If you've never served leeks or collard greens, or if you've always prepared venison in the same way, now is your chance to break out and investigate new ways and flavors.

Thanks to reliable home freezers and other preservation methods, the flavors of the wild wood can be served all year round. The herbs that add such flavor to nearly all our food, the woodsy tastes of mushrooms and wild game, and the strong, healthy flavors of greens can be enjoyed using the recipes in this chapter.

WILD HARVEST:

HEARTY MUSHROOM AND SAUSAGE PIZZA

CRUST:

3 cups flour

1 teaspoon sugar

1 tablespoon (1 packet) dry yeast

1 cup warm water (115° F)

1/2 teaspoon salt

2 tablespoons olive oil

1 tablespoon cornmeal

TOPPING:

1/2 pound bulk sausage

3 tablespoons olive oil

1/2 pound variety of fresh mushrooms, sliced thin

1 small onion, cut into thin rings

3 tomatoes, thinly sliced and seeded

1 clove garlic, finely chopped

1/2 pound mozzarella cheese, shredded

freshly ground black pepper and dried sage for garnish

Prepare the crust: In a food processor, mix 1 cup flour, sugar, and yeast. With processor running, add warm water. Turn processor off and add remaining 2 cups flour, salt, olive oil, and cornmeal. Process until mixture forms a ball. Sprinkle a 14-inch pizza pan with additional cornmeal, then pat dough onto the pan, forming a ridge around the edges. Heat oven to 500° F.

Prepare the topping: In a large skillet, brown the sausage well and drain all fat. Remove sausage and, in the same skillet, heat olive oil then sauté mushrooms and onion until onion is soft. Place tomato slices on pizza, then spread with sausage, mushroom/onion mixture, garlic, and top with cheese. Sprinkle generously with black pepper and sage. Bake 20 to 25 minutes or until crust is golden and cheese is melted and bubbly.

Makes 4 to 6 servings

Hearty Mushrooms and Sausage Pizza

MINNESOTA WILD RICE SOUP

1/2 ounce dried mushrooms

1 cup water

1 cup wild rice

4 cups water

1 tablespoon salt

1/4 cup butter or margarine

1 onion, finely chopped

2 cups fresh mushrooms, sliced

1/2 cup celery, chopped

1/4 cup flour

5 cups chicken stock

1 teaspoon dry mustard

1/2 teaspoon salt

2 cups milk or half-and-half

1/2 cup dry sherry, optional

fresh chives for garnish

The day before cooking the soup, soak the dried mushrooms in 1 cup water overnight. Drain the mushrooms and discard soaking water; chop mushrooms; set aside. Rinse the wild rice, then bring 4 cups water and 1 tablespoon salt to a boil in a large saucepan. Add rice and simmer, covered, 45 minutes. Drain rice in a fine sieve. In the same saucepan, melt butter and sauté onion for 5 minutes; add fresh mushrooms, celery, and dried mushrooms and sauté another 5 minutes. Mix in flour and stir until bubbly. Gradually add chicken stock, stirring constantly until slightly thickened. Stir in rice, mustard, and 1/2 teaspoon salt. Add milk and sherry, if using, and heat through but do not boil. Garnish each serving with chives.

Makes 6 to 8 servings

Now Murry brings back autumn crocuses and his handkerchief is full of mushrooms. I love the satiny color of mushrooms, & their smell & the soft stalk. The autumn crocuses push above short, mossy grass. . . . And I feel as I always do that autumn is loveliest of all. There is such a sharpness with the sweetness. . . .

KATHERINE MANSFIELD

MIXED MUSHROOM SAUTÉ

1/4 cup olive oil
1/4 cup butter or margarine
4 onions, cut into thin rings
2 cloves garlic, finely chopped
1 1/2 pounds variety of fresh mushrooms, thickly sliced
1/4 cup dry sherry or white wine

Mushrooms, appearing overnight, seemingly from nowhere, have long been surrounded by mystery in people's minds. Perhaps they were the result of thunder, since they often pop up after a thunderstorm. Or perhaps they mark areas where fairies dance in the forest. Or perhaps the ancient Greeks were right—they are the food of the gods.

In a large skillet, heat olive oil and butter or margarine; sauté onions and garlic until onions are golden; remove from skillet, leaving oil. In the same skillet, sauté the mushrooms, stirring often until the mushrooms have absorbed the oil and appear dry, then begin to give off moisture. Return the reserved onions to the skillet, add sherry or wine and heat to simmering; stir until sherry or wine is nearly evaporated.

Makes 6 to 8 servings

CREAMY GREEN SOUP

2 zucchini, chopped
2 carrots, chopped
1 celery stalk with some leaves, chopped
1 cup mushrooms, chopped
4 green onions, including some green part, chopped
6 cups chicken stock
6 cups Swiss chard, chopped
1 tablespoon fresh basil, chopped, or
1 teaspoon dried basil
1/2 teaspoon salt
1/2 teaspoon pepper
2 tablespoons fresh parsley, chopped

In a large saucepan or stock pot, combine the zucchini, carrots, celery, mushrooms, green onions, and chicken stock; bring to a boil, reduce heat, and simmer 30 minutes. Stir in the Swiss chard, basil, salt, pepper, and parsley. Simmer another 5 minutes. Serve as is or let cool slightly; then purée in a blender or food processor, a small amount at a time, then reheat before serving.

Makes 6 to 8 servings

Fresh, exotic mushrooms for
Mixed Mushroom Sauté, clockwise from center:
brown button, chanterelles, morels, and shitake

As for rosemary, I let it

run all over my garden

wall, not only because

my bees love it but

because it is the herb

sacred to remembrance

and to friendship,

whence a sprig of it

hath a dumb language.

SIR THOMAS MORE

WATERCRESS AND CUCUMBERS WITH WILDFLOWER HONEY DRESSING

DRESSING:

2/3 cup olive oil or vegetable oil
1/4 cup fresh lemon juice
1/4 cup white wine vinegar
2 tablespoons wildflower honey
2 teaspoons fresh rosemary, finely chopped, or
1/2 teaspoon dried rosemary
1/4 teaspoon salt

SALAD:

3 cups Boston lettuce leaves, torn into bite-size pieces
1 cup watercress
1/4 cup fresh parsley, chopped
1/2 English ("seedless, burpless") cucumber,
cut in half lengthwise then into thin slices
pomegranate seeds or fresh raspberries for garnish,
if desired

Prepare the dressing: In a jar with a tight-fitting lid, shake all the dressing ingredients together until well blended; set aside.

Prepare the salad: On six cold salad plates, arrange the lettuce, watercress, and parsley, then top with the half-circles of cucumber. Pour dressing over the salads, then garnish lightly with pomegranate seeds or raspberries.

Makes 6 servings

FIELD GREENS
WITH
ROASTED PEPPER VINAIGRETTE

Field Greens to dress with Roasted Pepper Vinaigrette, top row, left to right: butter lettuce, chicory, romaine, and green leaf lettuce; bottom row: escarole, raddichio, arugula or rocket, and red leaf lettuce.

VINAIGRETTE:

1 red bell pepper

1/2 cup olive oil

1/3 cup white wine vinegar or balsamic vinegar

1/3 cup red onion, chopped

1 clove garlic, finely chopped

1/2 teaspoon salt

1/4 teaspoon pepper

SALAD:

2 cups romaine lettuce, torn into bite-size pieces

1 cup arugula, torn into bite-size pieces

1 cup radicchio, torn into bite-size pieces

1 head Belgian endive, cut crosswise into thin rings

3 tablespoons Parmesan cheese, finely grated

Prepare the vinaigrette: Heat the broiler and place the pepper on the rack of a broiler pan. Roast, turning often, until charred and blistered on all sides. Place the pepper in a paper bag to steam for 10 minutes, which will make it easier to peel. With a paring knife, pull off skin; core and seed the pepper and cut into slices. Place the pepper in a blender or food processor and blend with olive oil and vinegar until nearly smooth; pour into a small bowl. Stir pepper mixture with onion, garlic, salt, and pepper. Refrigerate until serving time.

Prepare the salad: Toss the lettuces together in a large salad bowl and, just before serving, add about 1/4 of the vinaigrette; toss thoroughly. Pass the remaining vinaigrette and cheese.

POTATO PANCAKES WITH HERBS

2 cups seasoned mashed potatoes
1/4 cup flour
6 eggs
1/4 cup chives, chopped
1/4 cup fresh parsley, chopped
vegetable oil
sour cream and additional chopped chives, optional

Early in the day, mix together the mashed potatoes and flour in a bowl. Beat in the eggs, one at a time, mixing thoroughly after each addition. Cover and refrigerate 6 hours. Stir in the chives and parsley. Heat 1/2 inch of oil in a large skillet to 350° F or until a bread cube sizzles and browns. Drop potato mixture into the hot oil by teaspoonsful, but don't allow it to dribble in. Drain on paper towels and keep warm until all pancakes are made. Serve with sour cream and chives, if desired.

LEEK TART

6 leeks, white part only, well washed and
cut crosswise into thin slices
1 cup boiling water
1 teaspoon salt
2 (3-ounce) packages light cream cheese
1 (13-ounce) can evaporated skim milk
1/3 cup low-fat milk
2 eggs, lightly beaten
1/8 teaspoon nutmeg
1 (9-inch) pie crust, unbaked

Heat oven to 325° F. Place leeks, water, and salt in a saucepan and simmer 10 minutes. Drain leeks in a fine sieve; set aside. In a saucepan, cream together the cream cheese, evaporated milk, and milk; heat until cheese is melted and smooth. Beat a small amount of milk mixture into eggs, then pour eggs into pan. Stir in leeks and nutmeg; pour into crust. Bake 45 to 50 minutes or until filling is set. Let cool 10 minutes before cutting.

Makes 6 servings

WHOLE WHEAT SALAD WITH LEMON AND HERBS

3 cups water
1 teaspoon salt
1 1/2 cups uncooked bulgur wheat
2 tomatoes, seeded and chopped
1/2 cup fresh lemon juice
3 tablespoons olive oil
1/4 cup fresh parsley, chopped
2 tablespoons chives, chopped
1 tablespoon fresh mint, chopped
1 clove garlic, finely chopped
shredded lettuce
2 avocados, peeled, pitted, and cut into thin slices

Early in the day, bring water and salt to a boil; stir in bulgur wheat, cover tightly, and remove from heat. Let steam 15 minutes, then refrigerate until chilled. Toss together bulgur wheat with tomatoes, lemon juice, oil, parsley, chives, mint, and garlic. Arrange shredded lettuce on eight cold salad plates and fan avocado slices on the sides of the plates. Spoon salad on lettuce.

Makes 8 servings

Some of nature's most glorious gifts grow beneath our feet—onions, garlic, shallots, potatoes, yams, celeriac, leeks, beets, turnips, carrots, peanuts—and some grow wild for the picking for those who know how to see.

Potato Pancakes with Herbs

SOULFUL GREENS

6 slices bacon
1 pound (about 6 cups) collard greens,
chopped with stems removed
1/4 cup water
1/2 teaspoon salt
2 hard boiled eggs, chopped

Cook bacon until crisp; remove from skillet and crumble; set aside. Leave 2 tablespoons bacon grease in the skillet and add collard greens, water, and salt. Cover and let steam for 10 to 15 minutes or until tender. Add bacon and eggs; toss and serve.

Makes 4 servings

PREPARING LETTUCES FOR STORAGE

To maximize the storage life of lettuces, take these simple steps as soon as you bring them in from the garden or market.

Lettuces and other greens with stalks, such as romaine and red leaf: Trim 1/8 inch off the bottom of the stalk then stand the lettuce in a bowl of lukewarm (not cold) water for 5 minutes to allow the lettuce to "drink." Immediately shake off any excess water and place the lettuce in an airtight plastic container or plastic bag; refrigerate. The shock of going into the cold refrigerator will make the lettuce very crisp. This also works for celery.

Head lettuces, such as iceberg and Boston: Remove the core of the lettuce. With strong lettuce, such as iceberg, you can bang the core end on the counter to loosen it, then pull the core out. Run lukewarm water into the bottom of the lettuce then shake it out. Place in an airtight plastic container or plastic bag and refrigerate immediately.

Soulful Greens

WILD GAME:

VENISON WITH CHERRIES

1/4 cup butter or margarine
3 pounds venison sirloin steak, cut 1 1/2-inches thick
1/4 cup flour
2 cups fresh cherries, pitted and halved
1 onion, cut into thin rings
1 cup cider vinegar
1 cup water
2 bay leaves
1 teaspoon salt
1/2 teaspoon pepper

Melt the butter or margarine in a large skillet with a lid. Dredge the venison in flour and brown on both sides. Add the cherries, onion, vinegar, water, bay leaves, salt, and pepper; cover tightly. Bring to a boil, then reduce heat and simmer very gently for 1 to 1 1/2 hours or until tender, checking toward the end of cooking and adding boiling water if sauce is too thick.

Makes 4 to 6 servings

VENISON SWISS STEAK

1/4 cup flour
1 teaspoon salt
1/8 teaspoon cayenne pepper
1/8 teaspoon nutmeg
1/8 teaspoon cloves
3 pounds venison round steak, cut 1 inch thick
1/4 cup butter or margarine
2 onions, cut into thin rings
1 (16-ounce) can tomatoes, undrained
1 tablespoon Worcestershire sauce
1 cup dry red wine
1 garlic clove, finely chopped
1/2 cup carrots, chopped
1/2 cup green bell pepper, chopped

Venison with Cherries

1/2 cup celery, chopped
1/2 cup fresh mushrooms, chopped

Heat oven to 350° F. In a shallow bowl, mix together the flour, salt, cayenne, nutmeg, and cloves. Pound the seasoned flour into the venison until the flour is completely absorbed. Cut the meat into strips 3-inches wide and 1/2-inch thick. Heat the butter or margarine in an oven-safe Dutch oven or large skillet with a lid and brown the meat; add onions and sauté another 3 minutes. Add the tomatoes with their liquid, Worcestershire sauce, wine, garlic, carrots, bell pepper, celery, and mushrooms. Cover tightly and bake 2 to 2 1/2 hours or until meat is very tender.

Makes 4 to 6 servings

DUCK WITH SAGE DRESSING

DUCK:

1 (4- to 5-pound) wild or farm-raised duck

1 tablespoon salt

DRESSING:

2 onions, chopped

1/2 cup water

1/4 cup melted butter or margarine

3 cups soft bread cubes

1 tablespoon fresh sage, chopped, or

1 teaspoon dried sage

1 teaspoon salt

Heat oven to 325° F. Prick the skin of the duck all over with a sharp fork, then rub well with salt to crisp the skin. Place on a rack, breast side up, in a shallow roasting pan. Roast for 2 1/2 hours, pricking the skin often during cooking to release excess fat. Meanwhile, make the dressing: Simmer the onion, butter, and water together, covered, for 20 minutes, or until the onion is tender. Mix in the bread cubes, sage, and salt. Spoon into a well-greased 1 1/2-quart baking dish. Bake, uncovered, for 1 hour.

Makes 4 servings

MARINADE FOR CHARBROILED GAME

This simple marinade tenderizes and cuts down the wild flavor in dove, venison, duck, or quail before it is grilled over charcoal or broiled in an oven.

1/2 cup butter or margarine

1/2 cup fresh lemon juice

1 tablespoon Worcestershire sauce

1 tablespoon soy sauce

Melt the butter, then add the remaining ingredients. Marinate game or birds, covered and refrigerated for 4 to 12 hours, depending on thickness of the meat. Baste meat frequently with marinade during cooking.

BRAISED QUAIL

2 cups flour

2 teaspoons salt

1/2 teaspoon pepper

12 quail, cleaned and dressed

1/2 cup butter or clear bacon drippings

2 cups beef stock

1/2 cup onion, chopped

1/2 cup celery, chopped

2 tablespoons cider vinegar or red wine vinegar

In a shallow bowl, mix together the flour, salt, and pepper. Roll the birds in the seasoned flour. Melt the butter or bacon drippings in a large skillet with a lid. Brown the birds in the fat, a few at a time. Fit all the browned birds in the skillet in one layer. Pour in beef stock and add onion, celery, and vinegar. Cover and bring to a boil, then reduce heat and simmer gently for 1 hour.

Makes 4 servings

BACON WRAPPED CORNISH HENS

2 Cornish game hens

4 slices bacon

1/4 cup Dijon mustard

1/4 cup pineapple juice

1/2 cup water

1/2 cup dry white wine

Heat oven to 325° F. Wrap each bird with 2 slices of bacon, securing with skewers or toothpicks. Mix together the mustard and juice, then brush it over the bacon. Place the birds breast side up on a rack in a shallow roasting pan and cover loosely with foil. Pour the water and wine into the pan. Roast 1 hour, then remove the foil and roast another 1/2 hour or until bacon is brown. Serve whole or remove back bone and butterfly on serving plate.

Makes 2 servings

Quail served with mashed turnips
and grains with currants and scallions

STEWED RABBIT

Cooking something delicious is really much more satisfactory than painting pictures or throwing pots. At least for most of us. Food has the tact to disappear, leaving room and opportunity for masterpieces to come.

JANE GRIGSON

1-inch square of fresh lemon rind
1 clove garlic
1 (3-pound) rabbit, cleaned, dressed, and cut up
1 slice bacon, chopped
1 onion, chopped
4 carrots, cut into chunks
1 stalk celery, chopped
1/4 cup fresh parsley, chopped
1 1/2 teaspoons salt
1/8 teaspoon nutmeg
1 cup water
1 cup milk
2 tablespoons flour blended in 1/4 cup water

Impale the lemon rind and garlic on a toothpick and put it in a Dutch oven or large saucepan with the rabbit, bacon, onion, carrots, celery, parsley, salt, nutmeg, water, and milk. Cover and bring to a boil, then reduce the heat and simmer very gently for 45 minutes to an hour or until rabbit is tender. Remove the lemon rind and garlic. Pour the flour/water mixture into the stew and stir until slightly thickened; let simmer 2 or 3 minutes before serving.

Makes 4 servings

RABBIT WITH MUSHROOMS

1 (3-pound) rabbit, cleaned, dressed, and cut up
1 teaspoon salt
1/2 teaspoon pepper
3 tablespoons olive oil
2 onions, chopped
1/4 pound bacon or salt pork, chopped
2 cups Riesling wine or chicken stock
1/2 pound fresh mushrooms, sliced
4 bay leaves
1/2 teaspoon dried thyme
1/2 cup soft bread crumbs
3 tablespoons Dijon mustard
1 tablespoon fresh parsley, chopped

Sprinkle the rabbit pieces with salt and pepper. Heat the oil in a large skillet and brown the rabbit on all sides; remove from skillet. In the same pan, sauté the onion and bacon or salt pork just until the onion is transparent. Add the rabbit, wine or stock, mushrooms, bay leaves, and thyme. Cover tightly and simmer very gently for 45 minutes to 1 hour or until rabbit is tender. Remove the rabbit to a warm serving platter and keep warm. In a food processor or blender, process the bread crumbs, mustard, and parsley together until crumbly, then stir into the stew juices and pour over the rabbit. This recipe can be made with chicken, if you like.

Makes 4 servings

FIELDS AND ORCHARDS

While many cakes and desserts are available in handy boxes and from grocers' freezers, there are many Americans who favor baking 'from scratch' to create their own family traditions and to entertain friends with homemade goodies. The discovery of a delicious new way to make a quick or yeast bread, or creating a dessert that has your family clamoring for more, or delivering a luscious peach pie to a friend are all very gratifying experiences for those who love good food and cooking.

America's bounty is especially evident in the fields and orchards that extend from coast to coast. Pure white or mealy brown flours milled from the wheat grown under the big skies of the Midwest, mixed with brown or white sugars that flow, pour, or pack, are often the beginnings of delightful additions to our menus. Add fruits of the field or orchard, including apples, peaches, figs, nuts, and berries, for down-home aromas and flavors that evoke memories of Grandma's generous heart and hearth.

Fruits and nuts served in desserts always add color and fabulous flavors—not to mention needed nutrients—to our meals. Consider the combination of contrasting colors such as those of lemon and blueberries or kiwi and raspberries; experience the warm aromas of baking ginger cookies and the flavor burst of tart apples baked in a flaky crust.

When you have the time, choose to make fresh baked bread and serve it warm from the oven, or when your time is crunched, whip up a quick-to-mix dessert—both styles of baking are offered here to fulfill your desires for homey warmth or speedy gratification.

CRUSTY SOURDOUGH LOAF

1 tablespoon (1 packet) dry yeast
3/4 cup warm (105° F) water
1/2 cup plain yogurt at room temperature
2 tablespoons vegetable oil
1 tablespoon sugar
3/4 teaspoon salt
2 to 2 1/2 cups bread flour or all-purpose flour
cornmeal

In a large bowl, dissolve the yeast in water. Stir in the yogurt, oil, sugar, salt, and 1 cup of flour; mix well. Continue to add flour until dough is stiff. Turn out onto a floured board and continue to add flour, mixing it in with your hands, until it is just slightly sticky. Knead 8 to 10 minutes or until the dough is smooth and elastic. Return the dough to the large bowl, cover, and let rise in a warm place 1 hour or until double in bulk. Turn out of the bowl and punch down.

With non-stick vegetable spray, coat thoroughly a large (at least a 2 1/2-quart) ceramic or metal casserole or Dutch oven with a lid; sprinkle the bottom lightly with cornmeal. Form the loaf by patting it into a circle like a pizza, then fold the edges into the center, forming a ball that will be smooth on the underside and lumpy on top; turn it smooth side up and place it in the casserole.

Heat the oven to 450° F 20 minutes before baking time. Cover the casserole loosely with foil and let rise again about 45 minutes or until double in bulk. Pour 1/4 cup warm water over the loaf, then slash a large X in the top of the loaf with a very sharp knife. Cover the pan with foil, then with the lid, so steam cannot escape. Bake 20 minutes, then open the oven door for a minute to reduce the heat and uncover the bread. Turn the thermostat down to 350° F and bake another 20 to 30 minutes or until nicely browned and the loaf sounds hollow when the bottom is tapped. Remove from the pan and let cool on a wire rack before slicing.

Makes one round loaf

Bread deals with living things, with giving life, with growth, with the seed, the grain that nurtures. It is not coincidence that we say bread is the staff of life.

LIONEL POILANE

MADISON COUNTY CHEESE BREAD

1 cup buttermilk or milk
1/2 cup water
1/4 cup onion, finely chopped (optional)
2 cups (about 8 ounces) sharp Cheddar cheese, finely shredded
2 tablespoons vegetable oil
2 tablespoons sugar
2 teaspoons salt
2 tablespoons (2 packets) dry yeast
1/3 cup warm (105° F) water
1 egg, lightly beaten
6 cups bread flour or all-purpose flour

Warm the atmosphere of your home to invite family and guests by creating a welcoming scent. Simply put orange rinds and cinnamon sticks in a pot of simmering water on the stove. Or, if you have some dried lavender or rose petals from your summer garden, toss them in the water instead.

Heat the buttermilk or milk, water, onion, if using, cheese, oil, sugar, and salt together until bubbles form around the edge of the pan. Let cool to lukewarm. Dissolve the yeast in warm water in a large bowl. Add the cooled cheese mixture, egg, and 3 cups of the flour. Mix well, then continue to add flour about 1/2 cup at a time until too thick to stir. Turn out onto a floured board and continue to add flour, mixing it in with your hands, until it is just slightly sticky. Knead 8 to 10 minutes or until the dough is smooth and elastic. Return the dough to the bowl, cover, and let rise in a warm place 1 hour or until double in bulk. Turn out of the bowl and punch down. Cover with the inverted bowl and let rest 10 minutes.

Turn dough out and cut in half. Shape loaves by patting out into 9-inch squares; roll up jelly-roll fashion and pinch the edge to seal. Pull the ends under the loaf to create smooth ends. Place in 2 greased 9- x 5-inch loaf pans; cover loosely and let rise about 45 minutes or until double in bulk. Heat oven to 375° F 20 minutes before baking time. Bake 30 to 40 minutes or until nicely browned and the loaf sounds hollow when the bottom is tapped. Remove from the pan and let cool on a wire rack before slicing. If you like a shiny dark crust, brush the tops with an egg yolk beaten with 1 tablespoon water just before baking.

Makes 2 large loaves

NEW MEXICAN CORNBREAD

1 cup cornmeal
1 cup flour
3 tablespoons sugar
1 tablespoon baking powder
1 teaspoon crushed red pepper flakes
1 (17-ounce) can creamed corn
1/2 cup milk
1/4 cup vegetable oil
1/4 cup onion, grated or finely chopped
1 egg

Heat oven to 375° F. In a large bowl, stir together the cornmeal, flour, sugar, baking powder, and red pepper. In another bowl, beat together the corn, milk, oil, onion, and egg. Pour the corn mixture into the dry mixture and mix together lightly, just to moisten. Spread in a well-greased 8- x 8-inch baking pan. Bake 25 to 30 minutes or until golden brown and a toothpick inserted in the center comes out clean.

Makes an 8- x 8-inch loaf

WEST VIRGINIA SPOONBREAD

2 cups milk
3/4 cup white cornmeal
3 tablespoons butter or margarine
2 teaspoons sugar
1 teaspoon salt
3 eggs, separated

Heat oven to 300° F. In a saucepan, heat milk until bubbles appear around the edges of the pan. Add cornmeal and cook over medium-low heat, stirring constantly, until thick. Add butter or margarine, sugar, and salt. Set aside to cool slightly. Beat in egg yolks. In a small bowl, whip egg whites until stiff and fold into cornmeal mixture. Spread in a well-greased 1 1/2-quart baking dish and bake 45 to 55 minutes or until set. Serve with butter.

Makes 4 to 6 servings

PUMPKIN-ORANGE BREAD

1 (16-ounce) can solid-pack pumpkin

3/4 cup vegetable oil

1/2 cup orange juice

3 eggs

2 1/2 cups flour

2 cups sugar

1 tablespoon orange rind, finely shredded

1 1/2 teaspoons baking soda

1 teaspoon salt

1 teaspoon cinnamon

1 teaspoon nutmeg

1/2 teaspoon cloves

1 cup walnuts, chopped (optional)

Heat oven to 350° F. In a large mixing bowl, beat together the pumpkin, oil, juice, and eggs. In another bowl, stir together the flour, sugar, orange rind, baking soda, salt, cinnamon, nutmeg, cloves, and walnuts, if using. Pour the dry ingredients into the pumpkin mixture and blend well. Pour into 2 well-greased 9- x 5-inch loaf pans or a 10-inch Bundt or tube pan. Bake 60 to 70 minutes for loaves, or 70 to 75 minutes for tube cake, or until a toothpick inserted in the center comes out clean. Let cool in the pan 15 minutes, then turn out onto a wire rack to cool completely.

Makes 2 loaves or 1 tube cake

LIGHTENING PIE

1 (14-ounce) can sweetened condensed milk

1 (6-ounce) can lemonade concentrate,
thawed and undiluted

3 cups frozen non-dairy whipped topping, thawed

1 (9-inch) graham cracker crust

Beat together the sweetened condensed milk and lemonade. Fold in the whipped topping; pour into crust and refrigerate at least 4 hours or overnight. Top with additional whipped topping before serving, if you like.

Makes 6 to 8 servings

SWEET AND TART APPLE PIE

1 (9-inch) double pie crust
6 or 7 Granny Smith apples, peeled, cored,
and cut into 1/4-inch slices
1/3 cup moist dried apricots, slivered
2 teaspoons lemon juice
1 cup sugar
1/4 teaspoon cinnamon
1/4 teaspoon nutmeg
1/4 teaspoon salt
2 tablespoons butter or margarine

Heat oven to 425° F. Fit the bottom crust in a 9-inch pie plate; set crusts aside. In a large bowl, toss together apple slices, apricot slivers, and lemon juice. In a small bowl, stir together sugar, cinnamon, nutmeg, and salt; pour over apples and toss lightly but thoroughly. Arrange in the pie crust, then dot with butter. Brush rim of pastry with cold water, then fit top crust over apples and pinch edges to seal crusts together. Cut steam holes in the top crust. For a shiny crust, brush with milk and dust with sugar, if you like. Bake 15 minutes, then reduce heat to 350° F and bake another 30 to 35 minutes or until crust is light brown and filling is bubbly.

Makes 6 to 8 servings

FRESH PEACH PIE

1 cup sugar
4 tablespoons peach-flavored gelatin
3 tablespoons cornstarch
1 cup water
4 peaches, peeled, pitted, and sliced
1 (9-inch) pie shell, baked and cooled

In a saucepan, stir together the sugar, gelatin, and cornstarch. Gradually stir in the water and cook over medium heat, stirring constantly, until boiling; set aside to cool. Stir the peaches into the cooled gelatin then pour into the pie shell. Refrigerate at least 4 hours and serve with whipped cream, if you like.

Makes 6 to 8 servings

Sweet and Tart Apple Pie

We eat with our eyes before we taste. Make a small gift of jam or bread from your kitchen especially gorgeous by wrapping it in colored plastic wrap or netting and a metallic-sparkly ribbon. Or wrap the gift in plain brown paper, tie it with a jute string or plaid ribbon and embellish with dried herbs inserted in the knot.

CRANBERRY BUNDT CAKE

1 1/4 cups sugar
5 eggs
1 cup butter, melted
1 cup whole-berry cranberry sauce
1/2 cup sour cream
2 1/2 cups flour
1 tablespoon cinnamon
1 tablespoon ginger
2 1/2 teaspoons baking soda
1 teaspoon cloves

Heat oven to 350° F. In a large bowl, beat together the sugar and eggs until thick and pale. Stir in the butter, cranberry sauce, and sour cream. In a another bowl, stir together the flour, cinnamon, ginger, baking soda, and cloves; add to the cranberry mixture and blend well. Pour the batter into a well-greased 12-cup Bundt pan or tube pan. Bake 50 to 60 minutes or until a toothpick inserted in the center comes out clean. Let cool in the pan 15 minutes, then turn out onto a wire rack to cool completely.

Makes 1 cake

LEMON CREAM WITH BLUEBERRIES

2/3 cup sugar
7 tablespoons cornstarch
1/4 teaspoon salt
3 1/2 cups milk
1/2 cup fresh lemon juice
1 teaspoon lemon zest, finely shredded
1 drop yellow food coloring
1 teaspoon vanilla
1 cup fresh blueberries

Mix together the sugar, cornstarch, and salt in the top of a double boiler. Gradually stir in the milk, lemon juice, zest, and food coloring. Set over simmering water and stir constantly until thickened. Continue to cook 5 minutes, stirring occasionally. Remove from heat and stir in vanilla. Rinse a 5-cup ring mold with cold water then pour lemon mixture into it. Refrigerate for 4 hours or overnight. Unmold onto serving plate and scatter with blueberries.

Makes 6 to 8 servings

I was brought up to

believe no meal could

be eaten indoors if it

was possible to be

eaten outside, in the

garden, on a balcony

or wherever the sky

was all around.

LESLEY BLANCH

BLUEBERRY CRUMBCAKE

TOPPING:

1/2 cup packed brown sugar

3 tablespoons flour

2 teaspoons cinnamon

1/2 teaspoon nutmeg

1/4 teaspoon salt

3 tablespoons butter

CAKE:

1/4 cup butter

3/4 cup sugar

1 egg

2 cups flour

2 teaspoons baking powder

1/2 teaspoon salt

1/2 cup milk

2 cups blueberries, fresh or frozen (not thawed)

Prepare the topping: With a fork, toss together the brown sugar, flour, cinnamon, nutmeg, and salt; blend in the butter until crumbly. Set aside.

Prepare the cake: Heat the oven to 375° F. Cream the butter until fluffy, then add the sugar and egg and continue blending until light. In another bowl, stir together the flour, baking powder, and salt; add to creamed mixture with the milk and blend well as mixture will be thick. Gently fold in the blueberries, being careful not to break them. Spread in a greased 10-inch spring-form pan. Sprinkle the topping crumbs over the batter and bake 45 to 50 minutes or until a tooth-pick inserted in the center comes out clean.

Makes 8 servings

Blueberry Crumb Cake

FRUIT-TOPPED CHEESECAKE

CRUST:

3 cups gingersnap or vanilla wafer, very fine crumbs

1/3 cup butter, melted

FILLING:

3 (8-ounce) packages cream cheese, at
room temperature

1 cup sugar

3 eggs

2 teaspoons vanilla

2 teaspoons lemon zest, finely shredded or

1 teaspoon lemon extract

TOPPING:

4 kiwi fruit, peeled and sliced

2 fresh peaches, peeled, pitted, and sliced

1 cup raspberries, blueberries, or strawberries, or

mix 1/2 cup red currant jelly

Prepare the crust: With a fork, blend together the crumbs and butter. Press tightly into the bottom of a 9-inch springform pan; set aside.

Prepare the filling: Heat oven to 350° F. Beat the cream cheese until smooth then beat in sugar, eggs, vanilla, and lemon zest or extract. Pour into crust and bake 45 minutes. Turn off oven and let cool without moving for an hour. Refrigerate at least 4 hours or overnight.

Prepare the topping: Remove the side of the pan. Arrange the kiwi fruit around the edge of the cheesecake then make another circle of peach slices, slightly overlapping the kiwi. Make a pile of berries in the center, scattering a few over the other fruit. Melt the jelly, but don't let it boil. Pour over the fruit and refrigerate until set.

Makes 8 to 10 servings

LEFT:
Fruit-Topped
Cheesecake with
optional topping ideas

RASPBERRY SQUARES

1/2 cup butter, at room temperature
1/2 cup packed brown sugar
1 cup flour
1/4 teaspoon baking soda
1 cup quick-cooking or regular oats
3/4 cup seedless raspberry jam

Heat oven to 350° F. Line an 8- x 8-inch baking pan with foil then butter the foil. Mix together the butter, brown sugar, flour, baking soda, and oats. Press 2 cups of the oat mixture into the pan. Spread jam to within 1/4 inch of edges. Sprinkle with remaining crumbs, pressing lightly. Bake 30 to 35 minutes. Cool thoroughly before cutting.

SWEET AND SOUR PRUNES

You'll find many occasions to serve these "pickled" prunes—as a dessert with cheesecake or pound cake, as part of a fruit salad, or to accompany cheese, paté, sausages, ham, or turkey. They keep well in the refrigerator for several weeks.

1 pound prunes, or substitute dried apricots, figs, peaches, or pears

1 cup water

1/2 cup balsamic vinegar, or 1 cup red wine vinegar

1/2 cup sugar

8 cloves

4 cinnamon sticks or 1 teaspoon cinnamon

Put the dried fruit in a sterilized jar then add the remaining ingredients. Cover the jar and shake gently to help the sugar dissolve. Refrigerate at least 24 hours before serving.
Makes about 1 pint

It will be a special dinner. A sense of well-being has come over us in this land of plenty.

ROBERT BYRON

NUTTY SHORTBREAD

1 cup unsalted butter, at room temperature

1/2 cup powdered sugar

2 teaspoons vanilla

2 cups flour

1 cup cornstarch or potato starch flour

1/2 cup almonds, ground or finely chopped

1/2 cup walnuts or pecans, ground or finely chopped

Heat oven to 350° F. Cream the butter, sugar, and vanilla together. Add the flour and starch gradually, blending well. Turn out and knead vigorously until satiny smooth then blend in the nuts with your hand. Cut dough in half and pat each half into a 9-inch pie or cake pan. With the tines of a fork, mark each circle into 12 wedges. Bake 25 minutes or until pale gold then cool in pans 10 minutes. Carefully cut along the dotted lines into wedges and leave to cool completely. Store in tightly covered tins for at least 3 days before serving.

Makes 2 dozen cookies

BIG, SOFT GINGER COOKIES

1/2 cup butter or margarine

1 cup packed brown sugar

2 eggs

1 cup buttermilk

1 cup molasses or dark corn syrup

4 cups flour

2 teaspoons ginger or more to taste

2 teaspoons baking powder

1 teaspoon baking soda

1 teaspoon salt

1 teaspoon cinnamon

1 teaspoon nutmeg

1/2 teaspoon cloves

1 cup raisins or currants (optional)

1 cup nuts or sunflower seeds (optional)

Heat oven to 350° F. Cream the butter then add the sugar, eggs, buttermilk, and molasses or syrup; mix well. In another bowl, stir together the flour, ginger, baking powder, baking soda, salt, nutmeg, cloves, and raisins and nuts, if using. Blend dry ingredients into the creamed mixture. Drop by teaspoonsful onto a greased cookie sheet. Bake 12 to 15 minutes or until golden and set.

Makes about 6 dozen cookies

INDEX